SERMONS IN
TIMES OF CRISIS

SERMONS IN TIMES OF CRISIS

*Twelve Homilies
to Stir Your Soul*

With an Introduction and Commentary by
REV. PAUL D. SCALIA

TAN Books
Charlotte, North Carolina

If not noted below, text of sermon was taken from a public domain source and freely adapted.

Sermons by Ambrose, Chrysostom, and Leo revised and edited by Kevin Knight for www.newadvent.org. Used with permission.

Charles Borromeo: Selected Orations, Homilies and Writings, (Cihak, John R. ed. Santogrossi, Ansgar (tr.), T & T Clark, 2017. Used with permission.

The version of Saint Edmund *Challenge to the Privy Council* appeared in *This Rock* magazine, a publication of Catholic Answers, in 1994. Used with permission.

Jacques-Bénigne Bossuet: *On Preaching the Gospel,* Translation by Christopher Blum. Used with permission.

Blessed John Henry Cardinal Newman: *The Second Spring,* www.newmanreader.org. Used with permission.

Blessed Clemens Cardinal von Galen: *Against Euthanasia,* Translation by Daniel Utrecht of the Oratory for his biography of the cardinal entitled *Lion of Münster* (TAN Books, 2017). Used with permission.

Blessed Jerzy Popieluszko's sermon at the Mass for the Homeland courtesy of a website in his honor maintained by the Polish Institute of National Remembrance. https://popieluszko.ipn.gov.pl/xje/documents/sermons/432,The-Sermon-of-25-September-1983.html

Sermons by Pope St. John Paul II and Joseph Cardinal Ratzinger and all other excerpts from papal homilies, messages, and encyclicals in Father Scalia's introduction or comments copyright © Libreria Editrice Vaticana. All rights reserved. Used with permission.

Unless otherwise noted, or in the texts of the sermons themselves, Scripture quotations are from the Revised Standard Version of the Bible—Second Catholic Edition (Ignatius Edition). Copyright © 2006 Division of Christian Education of the National Council of the Churches of Christ in the United States of America. Used by permission. All rights reserved.

Excerpts from the English translation of the Catechism of the Catholic Church for use in the United States of America © 1994, United States Catholic Conference, Inc.—Libreria Editrice Vaticana. Used with permission.

Cover design by Caroline K. Green

ISBN: 978-1-5051-0878-1

Published in the United States by
TAN Books
PO Box 410487
Charlotte, NC 28241
www.TANBooks.com
Printed in the United States of America

PRESENTED TO

_____

Name

_____

Date / Occasion

Personal Note

_____

_____

_____

_____

_____

_____

_____

_____

CONTENTS

PUBLISHER'S NOTE

I⊤ IS AN honor for us here at TAN Books to present this magnificent collection of *Sermons in Times of Crisis* to our readers, as it is to have worked with Father Paul Scalia on the project. We also particularly would like to thank those who graciously granted us permission to use the versions of the sermons included within. They include T & T Clark (Borromeo), Catholic Answers (Campion's Brag), the Newman Reader www.newmanreader.org (Newman), Libreria Editrice Vaticana (John Paul II and Benedict), and Kevin Knight at www.newadvent.org for his gracious permission to use his versions—slightly modified from a nineteenth-century collection of the writings of the Church Fathers—of Ambrose, Chrysostom, and Leo. And, of course, we would like to thank the authors of original translations, Christopher Blum, Father Daniel Utrecht of the Oratory, and Father Ansgar Santogrossi, OSB.

Some of the entries, particularly those of the Church Fathers, *Campion's Brag*, and Newman's, do not make for easy reading as most of these are long and the English may, in some cases, seem unfamiliar to the modern ear. That

choice, to leave them largely as we found them, was deliberate, as we feel that much of the rhetorical force of the sermons is captured through reading them in their entirety in
the older English. It was an edifying project for us to work
on, and we hope the same will hold true for readers. It is
also our hope that our beloved priests and bishops will find
inspiration and encouragement in the words of these great
orators of God, and that they will be fortified, for they, too,
must preach sermons in a time of crisis.

ACKNOWLEDGMENTS

THIS PROJECT HAS been in the works for far longer than John Moorehouse at TAN Books would like to consider. I want to thank him for his counsel, suggestions, and especially his patience. For their ideas, suggestions, cautions, edits, and most of all for their priestly counsel, I thank Father Paul Check, Father Carter Griffin, and Father Gary Selin. Finally, I am especially indebted to Christopher Blum of the Augustine Institute for his translation of the Bossuet sermon done specifically for this book.

INTRODUCTION

Rev. Paul D. Scalia

AT ONE POINT in their frequent confrontations with Jesus, the chief priests and scribes sent officers to arrest him in the Temple. Those unfortunate men returned to their superiors empty-handed. When asked why they had not brought in the rabbi from Galilee, they explained in a tone of awe, "No man ever spoke like this man!" (Jn 7:46). That wonder characterizes the reaction to our Lord's preaching from start to finish. At the beginning of his public ministry, after that first sermon on a hillside in Galilee, the crowds "were astonished at his teaching" (Mt 7:28–29). And in his final days, the crowd was again "astonished at his teaching" (Mt 22:33)—nor did anyone "dare to ask him any more questions" (Mt 22:46).

No man ever spoke like this man. Nor has any man since. Of course, this is a theological truth before all else. This man spoke perfectly because he is also God. The perfection of Jesus's words came not from any special training or method but from himself, the Incarnate Word. As God, he speaks the truth in its fullness. As perfect man, he lacks nothing in his manner of speaking. As the one who alone is fully divine and fully human, Jesus Christ perfectly unites the truth of God and the words of men. His sacred humanity is the instrument of the divinity, expressing divine truths in human words.

Further, he possesses a perfect union with his words. Every speaker must be in union with the truth he conveys to some degree or another. The greater the union, the more convincing his words; the lesser the union, the less convincing. Only in Jesus Christ, the Word made flesh, do we encounter the perfect unity of speaker and message. He is both the Word speaking and the Word spoken; the Truth proclaiming and the Truth proclaimed. *No man ever spoke like this man* because no man ever possessed such oneness with the truth he conveyed.

In him, we encounter an important scholastic maxim at work: *whatever is received is received according to the mode of the receiver.* We learn according to our capacity to receive instruction. Which also means that we speak (or should) to others according to their ability to receive. We adapt our speaking to the capacity of the hearer, for it makes no sense to speak in a manner the recipient cannot grasp. Of course, this is the principle of the Incarnation itself. Without ceasing to be God, the Son makes himself entirely present and accessible to man. He proportions himself, so to speak, to us and comes to us in a manner in which we can receive him.

His preaching was one dimension of this divine pedagogy. He spoke to us in a way that we could receive—in a human manner, with the language, images, phrases, and expressions of that particular time, place, and people. His human words were the means by which divine truths came to their—and our—hearts and minds. "The Word, in Himself, expresses the infinite perfection of the Father, but as man, it is in human language adapted to our puny intelligence that He reveals to us the secrets of this divine life."[1]

No man ever spoke like this man. And this man desires to continue speaking. He wants to extend his proclamation of the kingdom. That is why Jesus commissioned his disciples to proclaim the Gospel: "Go into all the world and preach the gospel to the whole creation" (Mk 16:15). It is not simply that they preach about him. He himself proclaims the Gospel through them. "He who hears you hears me" (Lk 10:16). "As the Father has sent me, even so I send you" (Jn 20:21). These words to the first preachers apply to all commissioned to preach in his name. He desires that he himself be heard and received through them; that through their words, his Gospel be made present and effective in every time and place, in every culture and society, in every nation and land.

"The word of God is not chained" (2 Tm 2:9). This means that preaching the word of God must be the first duty of the Church's ministers. Unless we have preachers, we will not know Christ. "How are men to call upon him in whom they have not believed? And how are they to believe

---

[1] Blessed Marmion, *Christ the Ideal Priest*, trans. Matthew Dillon (Herefordshire: Gracewing, 2005), 195.

in him of whom they have never heard? And how are they to hear without a preacher? . . . Faith comes from what is heard. And what is heard comes by the preaching of Christ" (Rom 10:14, 17).

But what does this preaching—and the preacher—look like? To help our understanding of the preacher's vocation and office, we can avail ourselves of three images from Scripture. First of all, the prophet. The Old Testament prophets—those strange, often off-putting, characters—are the preacher's obvious predecessors. Their role in ancient Israel foreshadows and corresponds to the Church's prophetic office, of which preaching is the highest expression.

The Hebrew word for prophet, *nabi*, comes from a root meaning "to bubble forth, as from a fountain." This suggests that the prophet's words came—bubbled forth—from *within* him. He was no mere messenger. He first interiorized the word and, having thus established a certain unity with it, spoke. This provides an initial lesson about the Christian preacher. Like the prophet, he is no mere conveyer of information. He must first interiorize the Gospel, allow it to become part of him, and then speak out of the abundance of his heart. Anything less makes him not a Christian preacher but merely a human orator, or a town crier.

A curious trait we often encounter in the prophets is reluctance. Jonah shows it in the extreme. He is not, however, so much an example of this reluctance as its parody; his story is amusing because there is some truth in it. Amos, Isaiah, and Jeremiah speak of their reluctance and thus reveal an important truth: their prophetic mission was not their idea. The prophets spoke not from a human but from the divine initiative. Their reluctance confirms that the message was not theirs but his. Each prophet spoke according to his own temperament, personality, and style, but the content was always the Lord's. So also the Christian preacher. Commissioned by the Church, not by his own will, he speaks not his own opinions but the Lord's truth. Despite any reluctance he might feel, he must be attentive and docile to the Lord's promptings to speak his truth as the people need to hear it.

This docility to the divine initiative also means that the prophets spoke different messages, at different times, and to different groups. Sometimes they rebuked and warned; other times they consoled and comforted. What determined the message was, again, not the prophet's temperament, opinion, or mood but the Spirit of God moving him to speak what the people needed at a given time. Just so, the Christian preacher, docile to the Spirit, will proportion his message to the needs of the people. They may indeed need to hear words of rebuke, but they could just as well need words of consolation. The preacher's prayer should be to speak not what he wants them to hear or what they want to hear but only what the Lord wants them to hear.

The popular imagination sees the prophets as soothsayers, strange men who predicted the future. Some prophets certainly confirmed this stereotype by speaking about what would occur in the days to come. But the principal concern of the prophets was actually not so much to proclaim the future to the Israelites as to remind them of the past. The prophets, deeply rooted in the history, traditions, liturgy, and scriptures of ancient Israel, sought to keep the Israelites faithful to the covenant, to what they had received, and to what the Lord had made them. Without this fidelity to their past, the Israelites had no future. Their forgetfulness was always their undoing. The prophets served as a memory for the Israelites. They constantly pointed the people back—to the covenant, its obligations, and its promises. "Look to the rock from which you were hewn!" (Is 51:1).

And yet the prophets were not nostalgic or trapped in the past. They were men of their own time and place. They dwelled among the very people to whom they spoke. They shared their lives and often their fate. The prophets' rootedness in the covenant of Israel made their message timeless; their presence in the here and now made it timely. It was precisely because they were grounded in the tradition of Israel that they could speak to the present moment without compromising the message. They both understood the contemporary situation and knew how to apply eternal truths to it.

The preacher of the Gospel is the Christian prophet *par excellence*. Like the prophets of old, he must be rooted in the past; that is, in the Church's Scriptures, Tradition, and Liturgy. Only then can he bestow upon his people their proper inheritance: knowledge of what God has done for them and what he has made them. Of course, the preacher must at times address current issues as they arise. But if he always seeks to be "contemporary" and "relevant," he will soon find himself dated and irrelevant. A preacher without roots has nothing to say to the present moment except what people already know. He must have a memory, roots deep in the Church. The entire purpose of the memory, in fact, is to bring the past forward to have an effect in the present. Which means that, like the prophets, the preacher should also live and minister in the present, in his own day and age. He should be so rooted in the Church and so present in the here and now that he can speak timeless truths in a timely manner.

Another apt image of the preacher is the shepherd. Through Jeremiah, the Lord promises that his teaching will come from shepherds: "I will give you shepherds after my own heart, who will feed you with knowledge and under-standing" (Jer 3:15). Notice that this verse speaks primarily about the preacher's *interior* life. The first requirement is not eloquence, learning, or technique but that he be a man after the Lord's own heart. After all, it is ultimately Jesus who guards and nourishes the flock. He alone is the Good Shepherd (Jn 10:11), the true "shepherd of Israel" (Ps 80:1). The pastor who teaches in his place must be a worthy image of him. A man can pastor the flock authentically only to the degree that he is in union with the Good Shepherd.

Two qualities needed by a shepherd are diligence and vigilance. Diligence for setting boundaries and establishing the sheepfold; vigilance against threats to the flock. For the preacher, this means diligence in preaching the full Gospel, even the "hard sayings" (cf. Jn 6:60), and vigilance against the errors that threaten his flock. In the ancient world, the hard sayings and "hot button" topics surrounded theological matters: principally the Trinitarian and Christological dogmas. Today, they center almost exclusively on moral issues: abortion, contraception, homosexual activity, divorce, et cetera. As such, they threaten people's lifestyle and comfort more directly, and for that reason, can be even more difficult to address. But a shepherd must do so.

It is of course possible that some pastors could err by addressing the difficult subjects too often. The excessive discussion of such topics only lessens their importance in people's minds and makes the Faith appear to be just a moral code. Pope Benedict warned against the constant engaging of such issues lest pastors "give the impression that we are moralists" or "make Christianity seem merely morality."

On the other hand, some pastors err by ignoring controversial topics. Fearing to appear divisive, they avoid anything that might challenge or discomfort the congregation. In pursuit of a false unity, they refuse to name or confront error. Pope Saint Gregory the Great applies to them Isaiah's condemnation: "They are all dumb dogs, they cannot bark" (Is 56:10). It is a bitter irony that remaining silent out of fear of being divisive simply lets in error that truly divides.

So, while a pastor should not obsess about controversies, neither can he remain silent about what threatens his flock. He must speak out, and for several reasons. First, and most obviously, to instruct the ignorant. Especially since most Catholics receive their understanding of the Catholic faith from the media, the Sunday homily becomes the opportunity to clarify what the Church *really* teaches, and thus (one hopes) to inoculate the faithful against modern myths.

Second, to convert sinners. There is grace in the preaching of true doctrine. The preacher should be fully convinced that "the word of God is living and active, sharper than any two-edged sword, piercing to the division of soul and spirit, of joints and marrow, and discerning the thoughts and intentions of the heart" (Heb 4:12). Even if the preacher might not be the most eloquent, Christ's doctrine still has the power to convict sinners, cut them to the heart (cf. Acts 2:37), and bring them to conversion.

Third, a pastor must preach the difficult teachings to confirm the just; that is, to strengthen and encourage those already striving. If those struggling to live the faith in a hostile culture never hear the truth proclaimed, they will easily grow discouraged. They may wonder from their pastor's silence if he supports them. A pastor's clear proclamation of the full Gospel, however, will bring them needed support. The warning not to "preach to the choir" only goes so far: even the choir needs encouragement at times. Related to this is the consolation a pastor brings to the repentant when he proclaims the "hard teachings." The repentant—those who, after perhaps many years of straying, have turned back to the Lord and the Church—still need to hear the truth proclaimed. They need to know that conversion from evil to good is worth proclaiming. They need to hear others warned against the mistakes they made.

Fourth, and perhaps most importantly, the preacher must proclaim the hard teachings *for his own sake*. "Woe to me if I do not preach the gospel!" (1 Cor 9:16). These words of Saint Paul express his sober awareness that he had been commissioned to proclaim the Gospel. But this truth holds for all shepherds of souls: they will be judged on whether or not they preached the full Gospel. To withhold saving doctrine from the faithful because of its difficulty or unpopularity is a grave failure in pastoral charity and thus places the priest's own soul in danger.

"Woe to me if I do not preach the gospel!" The preacher himself loses something when he fails to preach the fullness of the Gospel. Put differently, there is a benefit to the preacher when he does preach the hard teachings. Every time he does so, he invests himself more deeply in them. By proclaiming such things publicly, he burns a bridge and commits himself more firmly to the truth. And if he does not do so—if he remains silent out of cowardice or misplaced compassion—then he harms himself by distancing himself from the truth. Some preachers probably avoid the hard teachings because they doubt or disbelieve them. But maybe the reverse is also true: that some preachers grew to doubt or stopped believing those teachings because they never preached them. To paraphrase Archbishop Fulton Sheen, either a priest will preach according to what he believes or he will believe according to what he preaches.

In the end, however, a shepherd must lead his flock to green pasture. Preaching is not only, or even primarily, about defending the sheep. It is about feeding them. Defense against error is not an end in itself. It serves the higher good of nourishing the flock. A pastor should desire not just the safety of his flock but also—and even more—its growth in Christ. And for that, his sheep need nourishment. Thus the priest is exhorted at his ordination, "Let what you teach be nourishment for the People of God" (Roman Ritual). Not just interesting or entertaining but *nourishing*.

This nourishment is the saving doctrine of the Church. Obviously, preaching differs from catechesis. But a sermon or homily that fails to convey doctrinal truths does not actually nourish. It might be interesting, consoling, perhaps even inspiring—for a time. But it is ultimately junk food. What truly nourishes is the pure doctrine of Christ presented to the congregation so that they can understand their lives in light of it and shape them according to it. This is what the Apostle means when he describes Saint Timothy as "nourished on the words of the faith and of the good doctrine" (1 Tm 4:6). This is what the Church means when she describes us as "formed by divine teaching."

The error that plagues so much preaching is the notion that doctrine has nothing to say to people's lives, that somehow people can have faith without the truth of Christ. It is the modernist hostility to creeds and dogmas. According to the *Catechism of the Catholic Church*, there is "an *organic* connection between our spiritual life and the dogmas" (CCC 89; emphasis added). Thus silence on matters of doctrine (no matter how well intentioned) deprives the soul of what nourishes it. Put differently, authentic care of souls requires the proclamation of doctrine.

In addition to the prophet and the shepherd, Saint Paul provides a third image of the preacher: the ambassador.

"We are ambassadors for Christ, God making his appeal through us" (2 Cor 5:20). Now, an ambassador must live, in effect, in two locations. He is simultaneously from the country that sends him and in the country to which he is sent. Any compromise on one end or the other hurts his mission. He must maintain a knowledge and affection for his homeland such that he still identifies with it and longs to be there. If he loses sight of his own country, he cannot faithfully represent it. At the same time, he must truly dwell in the country of mission—seeking to know its people, history, and mores. Most of all, he must speak their language, for his entire mission is to communicate the message of his homeland in a language the people can understand.

Our Lord himself is of course the perfect ambassador, simultaneously present to his Father and to us. He is at once the Word of God, dwelling eternally in the Father's heart (Jn 1:18), and the Son of Man, the Word made flesh dwelling among us (Jn 1:14). He speaks whatever he hears from the Father, but he always does so in a human manner. His preachers should imitate him and seek to be good ambassadors: present both to the God who sends them and to the people to whom they are sent. Thus Saint Gregory the Great observes that true preachers "not only aspire in contemplation to the holy head of the Church, that is to the Lord above, but also descend in commiseration downward to His members."

As an ambassador, the preacher must be primarily *from* God. In fact, this describes the Lord's first preacher, John the Baptist: "a man sent from God" (Jn 1:6). The preacher's native habitat should be in God's presence, among the things of God. His first concern and starting point is to dwell with God more fully so as to know him personally and not just about him. He should maintain such an affection for his heavenly homeland that he desires to bring others there. This speaks once again of the importance of the preacher's interior life. Our Lord called the Apostles first "to be with him" and secondarily "to be sent out to preach" (Mk 3:14). Such should be the preacher's habit: first to be with him, and only then to preach. Failure to spend time with the Lord inevitably leads to a poverty of preaching. It produces an ambassador with no knowledge of his messenger and thus no message.

A preacher apart from God is like a drainpipe. He simply passes along the latest rainfall; that is, the latest trend in preaching, gospel commentary, or, more likely, the latest secular news and theories. People may find this entertaining, perhaps even interesting. But the pipe eventually runs dry. Such a preacher might know *about* God, as we might know about an historical personage. But the faithful need and desire a preacher who knows God personally, who is truly from him. The preacher from God is more like a reservoir. Because he dwells with the Lord, he has a depth from which he can draw at any time. He can speak to people not just about the worldly things they already know but about the eternal life they desire.

At the same time, the preacher must be, like an ambassador, truly *among* the people to whom he is sent. In that way, he comes to know their history, customs, language, et cetera. Most importantly, he comes to know the people themselves. He knows their struggles, difficulties, and blessings. He knows what they need to hear and can speak it to them in a manner they can receive. The disconnected preacher, who dwells apart and does not know them, inevitably uses language they can't understand, addresses questions they haven't asked, and neglects the needs they actually have.

The Apostle's image of the ambassador is most perfectly fulfilled by the parish priest. He is a man sent from God to be with the people and to form them by his preaching. Modern media enable a preacher to reach people with whom he otherwise has no contact, and often to great effect. But the parish priest, dwelling among his people, serving them daily, sharing their sorrows and joys, knowing their struggles, he remains the norm. His appointment from the bishop, far from an ecclesiastical formality, in fact sends him to serve the people in God's name. Present to them and sharing in their lives, he knows best how to speak the truth of Christ in the manner that they can receive. All the more reason, then, for him to deepen his union with the Father—to be more and more *from* God—and to give himself more generously to his people, to spend and be spent for their souls (cf. 2 Cor 12:15).

Despite the benefits of these figures, however, the Christian preacher cannot be fully understood by way of the prophet, shepherd, and ambassador. For the preacher of the Gospel is ultimately a *spiritual father*. Saint Paul writes to the Corinthians, "I became your father in Christ Jesus through the gospel" (1 Cor 4:15). Saint James states that God the Father "willed to give us birth by the word of truth" (Jas 1:18). These words from the Apostles indicate how preaching the Gospel differs from all other forms of public speaking. It seeks not only to instruct, convict, and inspire but to bring Christ's life to souls. Christian preaching is generative, bringing grace to the soul. And the preacher is an instrumental cause of that grace. He should thus desire that Christ be formed in his hearers (cf. Gal 4:19), that they conceive Christ in their souls and bring him to birth by their actions. By his preaching, a spiritual father is the Father's instrument to communicate life-giving words, to give new birth by the word of truth.

The qualities of the prophet, shepherd, and ambassador point to and find their fulfillment in spiritual fatherhood. The prophet, first of all, reminded the people of Israel who they were; the spiritual father *bestows* an identity on the children of God. Indeed, children always look to their father for their identity, to know where they came from and who they are. This is their rightful inheritance, their patrimony (*patris* + *munus*), and thus the father's duty. The Christian preacher must fulfill this duty of spiritual fatherhood because Christians, like the Israelites, suffer a forgetfulness of God, of his works, and therefore of who they are. They risk losing their identity as children of God and suffering, as Chesterton put it, "the degrading slavery" of being children of their age.

The image of the shepherd is likewise fulfilled in the reality of spiritual fatherhood. More than any shepherd cares for his flock, a father protects and nourishes his children. He protects them, of course, by refuting the errors that threaten the family. In so doing, he also trains his children to be intellectually vigilant themselves. A shepherd establishes the sheepfold, the place where his flock finds safety. So also a father frames and shapes the Christian life by his teaching. He sets the boundaries within which the children of God can grow secure. There he nourishes them with words of truth and by the grace his words impart.

Finally, a spiritual father is an ambassador of *the* Father. No man becomes a spiritual father by willing it. He receives that grace in ordination, when he is configured to the eternal Son of the Father. He is a fathered father. As such, he must return constantly in his prayer to be with the Father, the font of all fatherhood (cf. Eph 3:15). Unless he himself cultivates a sense of being a son of God, he will not be able to speak as a father to God's children.

The generative nature of Christian preaching means that it is intrinsically ordered toward the Church's sacraments. We find this in the first Christian sermon. After Saint Peter preaches on Pentecost, the crowd responds, "What shall we do?" He answers, "Repent, and be baptized" (Acts 2:37–38). This exchange was in effect the goal of his entire sermon: to provoke a conversion of heart and elicit a desire for the grace of the sacraments. There is grace in the preaching itself. But preaching's ultimate goal is to bring the people to a worthier reception of sacramental grace.

Therefore the privileged place for preaching is within the liturgy, and in particular the Mass. The proclamation of the Word of God is directed toward the faithful's reception of the Word made flesh in the Eucharist. A preacher's proclamation of the Word of God looks toward nourishing his people with Holy Communion. This is where the preacher is revealed most of all as a spiritual father. He first nourishes his children with the preached word and then, from the altar, nourishes them with the Body of Christ.

This volume presents sermons from throughout the Church's history. It would be bold, indeed foolhardy, to boast a collection of the best sermons. This book makes no such claim. These sermons do not necessarily represent either the greatest oratory or the highest theology (although examples of both can be found among them). Rather, as the title indicates, the criterion for selection was the faithful, convincing proclamation of the Word of God amid some crisis. The crises vary from theological to political, from ecclesiastical to cultural. Whatever the case, each sermon addresses a particular situation confronting the flock of Christ. Each one provides an example of a preacher applying the truth of Christ to a specific moment. He interprets the times in light of the Gospel and seeks to form his people according to it.

Every preacher in this volume provides a great example of a prophet, shepherd, and ambassador. These are men deeply united to the Word of God, from whom the truth of the Gospel bubbles forth as refreshment for the people. They demonstrate the diligence and vigilance of good shepherds—courageously defending their flocks and tenderly nourishing them with the Church's saving doctrine. They appear—then and now—as men from the Father, faithfully communicating him to his children. Most of all, each preacher included here shows himself to be a true spiritual father, who knows his children well, defends and nourishes them, and imbues them with the knowledge that they are children of God. In that, they establish the norm for all preaching, whether in times of crisis or not.

Not every sermon is preached in a time of crisis. Indeed, we should desire that the Word be proclaimed in an atmosphere of tranquility so that it can be interiorized more serenely and deeply. But just as the big game reveals an athlete's talent, so the crises in the Church's history reveal the greatness of her preachers or, rather, the greatness of the Spirit speaking through them.

Saint Ambrose of Milan

AGAINST AUXENTIUS

*Were you afraid that I should desert the Church
and forsake you in fear for my own safety?*

THE GREATEST CRISES faced by the Church are heresies:
crises of doctrine and truth. To be sure, moral crises do
tremendous damage. But so long as the sure and certain
light of truth shines, the faithful can find the path again. By
blinding them to the truth, heresies deprive the People of
God of even that.

Saint Ambrose of Milan was a great defender of the
true Faith during the crisis of the Arian heresy. His stal-
wart defense brought him into confrontation with even
the imperial court. In 386, Empress Justina demanded that
Ambrose surrender one of his basilicas to the Arian bishop
Auxentius. To prevent its seizure, Ambrose and the faithful
hastened to the building and occupied it for several days.
Ambrose made the most of this time, instructing his people

and leading them in the chanting of the Psalms and other sacred music. In so doing, he preserved the church building for orthodox Christians. More importantly, he formed the people themselves into a body devoted to the truth and capable of withstanding error. On Palm Sunday, as their resistance neared a successful end, he preached the following sermon to explain his position and to assure the people of his vigilance for the Church of God.

❖   ❖   ❖

ON THE GIVING UP OF THE BASILICAS

I SEE THAT you are unusually disturbed, and that you are closely watching me. I wonder what the reason is? Is it that you saw or heard that I had received an imperial order at the hands of the tribunes, to the effect that I was to go hence, whither I would, and that all who wished might follow me? Were you afraid that I should desert the Church and forsake you in fear for my own safety? But you could note the message I sent, that the wish to desert the Church had never entered my mind; for I feared the Lord of the universe more than an earthly emperor; and if force were to drag me from the Church, my body indeed could be driven out, but not my mind. I was ready, if he were to do what royal power is wont to do, to undergo the fate a priest has to bear.

Why, then, are you disturbed? I will never willingly desert you, though if force is used, I cannot meet it. I shall be able to grieve, to weep, to groan; against weapons, soldiers, Goths, my tears are my weapons, for these are a priest's defence. I ought not, I cannot resist in any other way. But to fly and forsake the Church is not my way; lest anyone should suppose I did so from fear of some heavier punishment. You yourselves know that I am wont to show respect to our emperors, but not to yield to them; to offer myself freely to punishment, and not to fear what is prepared for me.

Would that I were sure the Church would never be given over to heretics. Gladly would I go to the Emperor's palace, if this but fitted the office of a priest, and so hold our discussion in the palace rather than the church. But in the consistory Christ is not wont to be the accused but the judge. Who will deny that the cause of faith should be pleaded in the church? If any one has confidence let him come hither; let him not seek the judgment of the Emperor, which already shows its bias, which clearly proves by the law that is passed that he is against the faith; neither let him seek the expected goodwill of certain people who want to stand well with both sides. I will not act in such a way as to give any one the chance of making money out of a wrong to Christ.

The soldiers about us, the clash of the arms wherewith the church is surrounded, do not alarm my faith, but they disquiet me from fear that in keeping me here you might meet with some danger to your lives. For I have learned by now not to be afraid, but I do begin to have more fear for you. Allow, I beg you, your bishop to meet his foes. We have an adversary who assails us, for our adversary "the devil goes about, as a roaring lion, seeking whom he may devour," (1 Peter 5:8) as the Apostle said. He has received, no doubt, he has received (we are not deceived, but warned of this) the power to tempt in this way, lest I might perhaps by the wounds of my body be drawn away from the earnestness of my faith. You have read how the devil tempted holy Job in these many ways, and how at last he sought and obtained power to try his body, which he covered with sores.

When it was suggested that I should give up the vessels of the Church, I gave the following answer: I will willingly give up whatever of my own property is demanded, whether it is estates, or house, or gold, or silver— anything, in fact, which is in my power. But I cannot take anything away from the temple of God; nor can I give up what I have received to guard and not to give up. In doing this I am acting for the Emperor's good, for it would neither be right for me to give it up, nor for him to receive it. Let him listen to the words of a free-spoken bishop, and if he wishes to do what is best for himself, let him cease to do wrong to Christ.

These words are full of humility, and—as I think—of that spirit which a bishop ought to show towards the Emperor. But since "our contest is not against flesh and blood, but also" (which is worse) "against spiritual wickedness in high places," (Eph 6:12) that tempter the devil makes the struggle harder by means of his servants, and thinks to make trial of me by the wounds of my flesh. I know, my brethren, that these wounds which we receive for Christ's sake are not wounds that destroy life, but rather extend it. Allow, I pray, the contest to take place. It is for you to be the spectators. Reflect that if a city has an athlete, or one skilled in some other noble art, it is eager to bring him forward for a contest. Why do you refuse to do in a more important matter what you are wont to wish in smaller affairs? He fears not weapons nor barbarians who fears not death, and is not held fast by any pleasures of the flesh.

And indeed if the Lord has appointed me for this struggle, in vain have you kept sleepless watch so many nights and days. The will of Christ will be fulfilled. For our Lord Jesus is almighty, this is our faith: and so what He wills to be done will be fulfilled, and it is not for us to thwart the divine purpose.

You heard what was read today: The Savior ordered that the foal of an ass should be brought to Him by the apostles, and bade them say, if any one withstood them: "The Lord has need of him." (Lk 19:35) What if now, too, . . . He has commanded that foal to be brought to Him, sending forth those apostles, who, having put off their body, wear the semblance of the angels unseen by our eyes? If withstood by any, will they (the apostles) not say: "The Lord has need of him?" If, for instance, love of this life, or flesh and blood, or earthly intercourse (for perhaps we seem pleasing to some), were to withstand them? But he who loves me here, would show his love much more if he would suffer me to become Christ's victim, for "to depart and be with Christ is much better, though to abide in the flesh is more needful for you." (Phil 1:23) There is nothing therefore for you to fear, beloved brethren. For I know that whatever I may suffer, I shall suffer for Christ's sake. And I have read that I ought not to fear those that can kill the flesh. (Mt 10:28) And I have heard One Who says: "He that loses his life for My sake shall find it" (Mt 10:39).

Wherefore if the Lord wills, surely no one will resist. And if, as yet, He delay my struggle, what do you fear? It is not bodily guardianship but the Lord's providence that is wont to fence in the servant of Christ.

You are troubled because you have found the double doors open, which a blind man in seeking his chamber is said to have unfastened. In this you learn that human watchfulness is no defence. Behold! One who has lost the gift of sight has broken through all our defences, and escaped the notice of the guards. But the Lord has not lost the guard of His mercy. Was it not also discovered two days ago, as you remember, that a certain entrance on the left side of the basilica was open, which you thought had been shut and secured? Armed men surrounded the basilica, they tried this and the other entrance, but their eyes were blinded so that that could not see the one that was open. And you know well that it was open many nights. Cease, then, to be anxious; for that will take place which Christ commands and which is for the best.

And now I will put before you examples from the Law. Eliseus was sought by the king of Syria; an army had been sent to capture him; and he was surrounded on all sides. His servant began to fear, for he was a servant, that is, he had not a free mind, nor had he free powers of action. The holy prophet sought to open his eyes, and said: "Look and see

how many more are on our side than there are against us."
(2 Kgs 6:16) And he beheld, and saw thousands of angels.
Mark therefore that it is those that are not seen rather than
those that are seen that guard the servants of Christ. But
if they guard you, they do it in answer to your prayers: for
you have read that those very men, who sought Eliseus,
entered Samaria, and came to him whom they desired to
take. Not only were they unable to harm him, but they were
themselves preserved at the intercession of the man against
whom they had come.

The Apostle Peter also gives you an example of either
case. For when Herod sought him and took him, he was put
into prison. For the servant of God had not got away, but
stood firm without a thought of fear. The Church prayed
for him, but the Apostle slept in prison, a proof that he was
not in fear. An angel was sent to rouse him as he slept, by
whom Peter was led forth out of prison, and escaped death
for a time.

And Peter again afterwards, when he had overcome
Simon, in sowing the doctrine of God among the people,
and in teaching chastity, stirred up the minds of the Gentiles. And when these sought him, the Christians begged
that he would withdraw himself for a little while. And
although he was desirous to suffer, yet was he moved at
the sight of the people praying, for they asked him to save
himself for the instruction and strengthening of his people.
Need I say more? At night he begins to leave the town, and
seeing Christ coming to meet him at the gate, and entering
the city, says: "Lord, where are You going?" Christ answers:

"I am coming to be crucified again." Peter understood the divine answer to refer to his own cross, for Christ could not be crucified a second time, for He had put off the flesh by the passion of the death which He had undergone; since: "In that He died, He died unto sin once, but in that He lives, He lives unto God." (Rom 6:10)

So Peter understood that Christ was to be crucified again in the person of His servant. Therefore, he willingly returned; and when the Christians questioned him, told them the reason. He was immediately seized, and glorified the Lord Jesus by his cross.

You see, then, that Christ wills to suffer in His servants. And what if He says to this servant, "I will that he tarry, you follow Me," (Jn 21:22) . . . ? For if His desire was to do the will of His Father (Jn 4:34), so also is it His desire to partake of our sufferings. Did He not, to take an example from our Lord Himself—did He not suffer when He willed, and was He not found when He was sought? But when the hour of His passion had not yet come, He passed through the midst of those that sought Him, (Jn 7:30) and, though they saw Him, they could not hold Him fast. This plainly shows us that when the Lord wills, each one is found and taken, but because the time is put off, he is not held fast, although he meets the eyes of those who seek him.

And did not I myself go forth daily to pay visits, or go to the tombs of the martyrs? Did I not pass by the royal palace both in going and returning? Yet no one laid hands on me, though they had the intention of driving me out, as they afterwards gave out, saying, "Leave the city, and go where you will." I was, I own, looking for some great thing, either sword or fire for the Name of Christ, yet they offered me pleasant things instead of sufferings; but Christ's athlete needs not pleasant things but sufferings. Let no one, then, disturb you, because they have provided a carriage, or because hard words, as he thinks them, have been uttered by Auxentius, who calls himself bishop.

Many stated that assassins had been dispatched, that the penalty of death had been decreed against me. I do not fear all that, nor am I going to desert my position here. Whither shall I go, when there is no spirit that is not filled with groans and tears; when throughout the Churches Catholic bishops are being expelled, or if they resist, are put to the sword, and every senator who does not obey the decree is proscribed. And these things were written by the hand and spoken by the mouth of a bishop who, that he might show himself to be most learned, omitted not an ancient warning. For we read in the prophet that he saw a flying sickle. (Zech 5:1) Auxentius, to imitate this, sent a flying sword through all cities. But Satan, too, transforms himself into an angel of light, (2 Cor 11:14) and imitates his power for evil.

You, Lord Jesus, have redeemed the world in one moment of time: shall Auxentius in one moment slay, as far as he can, so many peoples, some by the sword, others by sacrilege? He seeks my basilica with bloody lips and gory hands. Him today's chapter answers well: "But unto the wicked said God: Wherefore do you declare My righteousness?" That is, there is no union between peace and madness, there is no union between Christ and Belial. (2 Cor 6:15)

You remember also that we read today of Naboth, a holy man who owned his own vineyard, being urged on the king's request to give it up. When the king, after rooting up the vines, intended to plant common herbs, he answered him: "God forbid that I should give up the inheritance of my fathers." (1 Kgs 21:3) The king was grieved, because what belonged by right to another had been refused him on fair grounds, but had been unfairly got by a woman's device. Naboth defended his vines with his own blood. And if he did not give up his vineyard, shall we give up the Church of Christ?

Was the answer that I gave then contumacious? For when summoned I said: God forbid that I should give up the inheritance of Christ. If Naboth gave not up the inheritance of his fathers, shall I give up the inheritance of Christ? . . . I answered as a bishop ought to answer: Let the Emperor act as an emperor ought to. He must take away my life rather than my faith.

But to whom shall I give it up? Today's lesson from the Gospel ought to teach us what is asked for and by whom it is asked. You have heard read that when Christ sat upon the foal of an ass, the children cried aloud, and the Jews were vexed. At length they spoke to the Lord Jesus, bidding Him to silence them. He answered: "If these should hold their peace, the stones will cry out." (Lk 19:40) Then on entering the temple, He cast out the money-changers, and the tables, and those that sold doves in the temple of God. That passage was read by no arrangement of mine, but by chance; but it is well fitted to the present time. The praises of Christ are ever the scourges of the unfaithful. And now when Christ is praised, the heretics say that sedition is stirred up. The heretics say that death is being prepared for them, and truly they have their death in the praises of Christ. For how can they bear His praises, Whose weakness they maintain. And so today, when Christ is praised, the madness of the Arians is scourged.

Invited, then, by these praises, Christ enters His temple and takes His scourge and drives the money-changers out of it. For He does not allow the slaves of money to be in His temple, nor does He allow those to be there who sell seats. What are seats but honours? What are the doves but simple minds or souls that follow a pure and clear faith? Shall I, then, bring into the temple him whom Christ shuts out? For he who sells dignities and honors will be bidden to go out. He will be bidden to go out who desires to sell the simple minds of the faithful.

Therefore, Auxentius is cast out. Mercurius is shut out. The portent is one, the names are two! That no one might know who he was, he changed his name so as to call himself Auxentius, because there had been here an Arian bishop, named Auxentius. He did this to deceive the people over whom the other had had power. He changed his name, but he did not change his falseness. He puts off the wolf, yet puts on the wolf again. It is no help to him that he has changed his name; whatever happens he is known. He is called by one name in the parts of Scythia, he is called by another here. He has a name for each country he lives in. He has two names already, and if he were to go elsewhere from here, he will have yet a third. For how will he endure to keep a name as a proof of such wickedness? He did less in Scythia, and was so ashamed that he changed his name. Here he has dared to do worse things, and will he be ready to be betrayed by his name wherever he goes? Shall he write the death warrant of so many people with his own hand, and yet be able to be unshaken in mind?

The Lord Jesus shut a few out of His temple, but Auxentius left none. Jesus with a scourge drove them out of His temple, Auxentius with a sword; Jesus with a scourge, Mercurius with an axe. The holy Lord drives out the sacrilegious with a scourge; the impious man pursues the holy with a sword.

Does he, a man full of blood and full of murder, dare to make mention to me of a discussion? He who thinks that they whom he could not mislead by his words are to be slain with the sword, giving bloody laws with his mouth, writing them with his hand, and thinking that the law can order a faith for man to hold. He has not heard what was read today: "That a man is not justified by the works of the law," (Gal 2:16) or "I, through the law, am dead to the law, that I may live unto God," (Gal 2:19) that is, by the spiritual law he is dead to the carnal interpretation of the law. And we, by the law of our Lord Jesus Christ, are dead to this law, which sanctions such perfidious decrees. The law did not gather the Church together, but the faith of Christ. For the law is not by faith, but "the just man lives by faith." (Gal 3:11) Therefore, faith, not the law, makes a man just, for justice is not through the law, but through the faith of

Christ. But he who casts aside his faith and pleads for that the claims of the law, bears witness that he is himself unjust; for the just man lives by faith.

Shall any one, then, follow this law, whereby the Council of Ariminum is confirmed, wherein Christ was said to be a creature. But say they: "God sent forth His Son, made of a woman, made under the law." (Gal 4:4) And so they say "made," that is, "created." Do they not consider these very words which they have brought forward; that Christ is said to have been made, but of a woman; that is, He was "made" as regards his birth from a Virgin, Who was begotten of the Father as regards His divine generation? Have they read also today, "that Christ redeemed us from the curse of the law, being made a curse for us"? (Gal 3:13) Was Christ a curse in His Godhead? But why He is called a curse the Apostle tells us, saying that it is written: "Cursed is every one that hangs on a tree," (Gal 3:13) that is, He Who in his flesh bore our flesh, in His body bore our infirmities and our curses, that He might crucify them; for He was not cursed Himself, but was cursed in you. So it is written elsewhere: "Who knew no sin, but was made sin for us, for He bore our sins, (2 Cor 5:21) that he might destroy them by the Sacrament of His Passion."

These matters, my brethren, I would discuss more fully with him in your presence; but knowing that you are not ignorant of the faith, he has avoided a trial before you, and has chosen some four or five heathen to represent him, if that is he has chosen any, whom I should like to be present in our company, not to judge concerning Christ, but to hear the majesty of Christ. They, however, have already given their decision concerning Auxentius, to whom they gave no credence as he pleaded before them day by day. What can be more of a condemnation of him than the fact, that without an adversary he was defeated before his own judges? So now we also have their opinion against Auxentius.

And that he has chosen heathen is rightly to be condemned; for he has disregarded the Apostle's command, where he says: "Dare any of you, having a matter against another, go to law before the unjust and not before the saints? Do you not know the saints shall judge the world?" (1 Cor 6:1-2) . . . You see, then, that what he has introduced is against the Apostle's authority. Do you decide, then, whether we are to follow Auxentius or Paul as our master?

But why speak of the Apostle, when the Lord Himself cries through the prophet: "Hearken unto Me, My people, you who know judgment, in whose heart is My law." (Is 51:7) God says: "Hearken unto Me, My people, you that know judgment." Auxentius says: You do not know judgment. Do you see how he condemns God in you, who rejects the voice of the heavenly oracle: "Hearken unto Me, My people," says the Lord. He says not, "Hearken, you Gentiles," nor does He say, "Hearken, you Jews." For they who had been the people of the Lord have now become the people of error, and they who were the people of error have begun to be the people of God; for they have believed in Christ. That people then judges in whose heart is the divine, not the human law, the law not written in ink, but in the spirit of the living God; (2 Cor 3:3) not set down on paper, but stamped upon the heart. Who then, does you a wrong, he who refuses, or he who chooses to be heard by you?

Hemmed in on all sides, he (Auxentius) betakes himself to the wiles of his fathers. He wants to stir up ill-will on the Emperor's side, saying that a youth, a catechumen ignorant of the sacred writings, ought to judge, and to judge in the consistory. As though last year when I was sent for to go to the palace, when in the presence of the chief men the matter was discussed before the consistory, when the Emperor wished to seize the basilica, I was cowed then at the sight of the royal court, and did not show the firmness a bishop should, or departed with diminished claims. Do they not remember that the people, when they knew I had gone to the palace, made such a rush that they could not resist its force; and all offered themselves to death for the faith of Christ as a military officer came out with some light troops to disperse the crowd? Was not I asked to calm the people with a long speech? Did I not pledge my word that no one should invade the basilica of the church? And though my services were asked for to do an act of kindness, yet the fact that the people came to the palace was used to bring ill-will upon me. They wish to bring me to this now again.

I recalled the people, and yet I did not escape their ill-will, which ill-will, however, I think we ought rather to tempt than fear. For why should we fear for the Name of Christ? Unless perchance I ought to be troubled because they say: "Ought not the Emperor to have one basilica, to which to go, and Ambrose wants to have more power than the Emperor, and so refuses to the Emperor the opportunity of going forth to church?" When they say this, they desire to lay hold of my words, as did the Jews who tried Christ with cunning words, saying: "Master, is it lawful to give tribute to Cæsar or not?" (Mt 22:17) Is ill-will always stirred up against the servants of God on Cæsar's account, and does impiety make use of this with a view to starting a slander, so as to shelter itself under the imperial name? And can they say that they do not share in the sacrilege of those whose advice they follow?

See how much worse than the Jews the Arians are. They asked whether He thought that the right of tribute should be given to Cæsar; these want to give to Cæsar the right of the Church. But as these faithless ones follow their author, so also let us answer as our Lord and Author has taught us. For Jesus seeing the wickedness of the Jews said to them: "Why do you tempt Me? Show Me a penny." When they had given it, He said: "Whose image and superscription has it?" (Mt 22:18) They answered and said: "Cæsar's." And Jesus says to them: "Render unto Cæsar the things that are Cæsar's, and to God the things that are God's" (Mt 22:21). So, too, I say to these who oppose me: "Show me a penny." Jesus sees Cæsar's penny and says: "Render unto Cæsar the things that are Cæsar's, and unto God the things that are God's." Can they in seizing the basilicas of the church offer Cæsar's penny?

But in the church I only know of one Image, that is the Image of the unseen God, of Which God has said: "Let us make man in Our image and Our likeness;" (Gen 1:26) that

Image of Which it is written, that Christ is the Brightness of His glory and the Image of His Person. (Heb 1:3) In that Image I perceive the Father, as the Lord Jesus Himself has said: "He that sees Me sees the Father." (Jn14:9) For this Image is not separated from the Father, which fact, indeed, has taught me the unity of the Trinity, saying: "I and My Father are One," (Jn 10:30) and again: "All things that the Father has are Mine." (Jn 16:15) Also of the Holy Spirit, saying that the Spirit is Christ's, and has received of Christ, as it is written: "He shall receive of Mine, and shall declare it unto you" (Jn 16:14).

How, then, did we not answer humbly enough? If he demand tribute, we do not refuse it. The lands of the Church pay tribute. If the Emperor wants the lands, he has the power to claim them, none of us will interfere. The contributions of the people are amply sufficient for the poor. Do not stir up ill-will in the matter of the lands. Let them take them if it is the Emperor's will. I do not give them, but I do not refuse them. They ask for gold. I can say: "Silver and gold I do not ask for." But they stir up ill-will because gold is spent. I am not afraid of such ill-will as this. I have dependents. My dependents are Christ's poor. I know how to collect this treasure. On that they may even charge me with this crime, that I have spent money on the poor! And if they make the charge that I seek for defence at their hands, I do not deny it; nay, I solicit it. I have my defence, but it consists in the prayers of the poor. The blind and the lame, the weak and the old, are stronger than hardy warriors. Lastly, gifts to the poor make God indebted to us, for it is written:

"He that gives to the poor, lends to God." (Prv 19:17) The guards of warriors often do not merit divine grace.

They declare also that the people have been led astray by the strains of my hymns. I certainly do not deny it. That is a lofty strain, and there is nothing more powerful than it. For what has more power than the confession of the Trinity which is daily celebrated by the mouth of the whole people? All eagerly vie one with the other in confessing the faith, and know how to praise in verse the Father, Son, and Holy Spirit. So they all have become teachers, who scarcely could be disciples.

What could show greater obedience than that we should follow Christ's example, "Who, being found in fashion as a man, humbled Himself and became obedient even unto death?" (Phil 2:7-8) Accordingly He has freed all through His obedience. If, then, He was obedient, let them receive the rule of obedience to which we cling, saying to those who stir up ill-will against us on the Emperor's side: "We pay to Cæsar what is Cæsar's, and to God what is God's." Tribute is due to Cæsar, we do not deny it. The Church belongs to God, therefore it ought not to be assigned to Cæsar. For the temple of God cannot be Cæsar's by right.

That this is said with respectful feeling for the Emperor, no one can deny. For what is more full of respect than that the Emperor should be called the son of the Church. As it is said, it is said without sin, since it is said with the divine favor. For the Emperor is within the Church, not above it. For a good emperor seeks the aid of the Church and does not refuse it. As I say this with all humility, so, also, I state it with firmness. Some threaten us with fire, sword, exile; we have learned as servants of Christ not to fear. To those who have no fear, nothing is ever a serious cause of dread.

A sufficient answer, then, seems to have been given to their suggestion. Now I ask them, what the Savior asked: "The baptism of John, was it from heaven or men?" (Lk 20:4) The Jews could not answer Him. If the Jews did not make nothing of the baptism of John, does Auxentius make nothing of the baptism of Christ? For that is not a baptism of men, but from heaven, which the angel of great counsel (Is 9:6) has brought to us, that we might be justified to God. Wherefore, then, does Auxentius hold that the faithful ought to be rebaptized, when they have been baptized in the name of the Trinity, when the Apostle says: "One faith, one baptism"? (Eph 4:5) And wherefore does he say that he is man's enemy, not Christ's, seeing that he despises the counsel of God and condemns the baptism which Christ has granted us to redeem our sins.

Saint John Chrysostom

FIRST HOMILY ON EUTROPIUS

*This is the season not for
judgment but for mercy.*

WE TYPICALLY UNDERSTAND the word *crisis* to indicate a bad situation. In fact, the original Greek indicates something more nuanced: a turning point or a time for decision—even an opportunity. Saint John Chrysostom encountered one such moment in 399 when the consul Eutropius ran to the Church of Saint Sophia seeking sanctuary from his enemies. Not long before, Eutropius had been nearly all-powerful at the imperial court. He had even advocated revoking the right to sanctuary or asylum in churches. Running afoul of the empress, however, he suddenly needed the very sanctuary he had sought to ban. Thus it was that he found himself clinging to the altar for dear life. So, with Eutropius crouched behind the veil at the altar and with a church full of people come to see the spectacle, Chrysostom seized the moment to proclaim Christ's mercy—even to the Church's enemies.

❧   ❧   ❧

ON EUTROPIUS, THE EUNUCH, PATRICIAN AND CONSUL

VANITY OF VANITIES, all is vanity—it is always seasonable to utter this but more especially at the present time. Where are now the brilliant surroundings of your consulship? Where are the gleaming torches? Where is the dancing, and the noise of dancers' feet, and the banquets and the festivals? Where are the garlands and the curtains of the theatre? Where is the applause which greeted you in the city, where the acclamation in the hippodrome and the flatteries of spectators?

They are gone—all gone: a wind has blown upon the tree shattering down all its leaves, and showing it to us quite bare, and shaken from its very root; for so great has been the violence of the blast, that it has given a shock to all these fibres of the tree and threatens to tear it up from the roots. Where now are your feigned friends? Where are your drinking parties, and your suppers? Where is the swarm of parasites, and the wine which used to be poured forth all day long, and the manifold dainties invented by your cooks? Where are they who courted your power and did and said everything to win your favour? They were all mere visions of the night, and dreams which have vanished with the dawn of day: they were spring flowers, and when the spring was over they all withered: they were a shadow which has passed away—they were a smoke which has dispersed, bubbles which have burst, cobwebs which have been rent in pieces.

Therefore, we chant continually this spiritual song—Vanity of vanities, all is vanity. For this saying ought to be continually written on our walls, and garments, in the market place, and in the house, on the streets, and on the doors and entrances, and above all on the conscience of each one, and to be a perpetual theme for meditation. And inasmuch as deceitful things, and maskings and pretence seem to many to be realities it behooves each one every day both at supper and at breakfast, and in social assemblies to say to his neighbour and to hear his neighbour say in return vanity of vanities, all is vanity.

Was I not continually telling you that wealth was a runaway? But you would not heed me. Did I not tell you that it was an unthankful servant? But you would not be persuaded. Behold, actual experience has now proved that it is not only a runaway, and ungrateful servant, but also a murderous one, for it is this which has caused you now to fear and tremble. Did I not say to you when you continually rebuked me for speaking the truth, I love you better than they do who flatter you? I who reprove you care more for you than they who pay you court? Did I not add to these words by saying that the wounds of friends were more to be relied upon than the voluntary kisses of enemies (Prv 27:6).

If you had submitted to my wounds, their kisses would not have wrought you this destruction: for my wounds work health, but their kisses have produced an incurable disease.

Where are now your cup-bearers, where are they who cleared the way for you in the market place, and sounded your praises endlessly in the ears of all? They have fled, they have disowned your friendship, they are providing for their own safety by means of your distress. But I do not act thus, nay in your misfortune I do not abandon you, and now when you are fallen, I protect and tend you. And the Church which you treated as an enemy has opened her bosom and received you into it; whereas the theatres which you courted, and about which you were oftentimes indignant with me have betrayed and ruined you. And yet I never ceased saying to you why doest thou these things? you are exasperating the Church, and casting yourself down headlong, yet you hurried away from all my warnings. And now the hippodromes, having exhausted your wealth, have whetted the sword against you, but the Church which experienced your untimely wrath is hurrying in every direction, in her desire to pluck you out of the net.

And I say these things now not as trampling upon one who is prostrate, but from a desire to make those who are still standing more secure; not by way of irritating the sores of one who has been wounded, but rather to preserve those who have not yet been wounded in sound health; not by way of sinking one who is tossed by the waves, but as instructing those who are sailing with a favourable breeze, so that they may not become overwhelmed. And how may this be effected? By observing the vicissitudes of human affairs. For even this man had he stood in fear of vicissitude would not have experienced it; but whereas neither his own conscience, nor the counsels of others wrought any improvement in him, do ye at least who plume yourselves on your riches profit by his calamity: for nothing is weaker than human affairs. Whatever term therefore one may employ to express their insignificance it will fall short of the reality; whether he calls them smoke, or grass, or a dream or spring flowers, or by any other name; so perishable are they, and more naught than nonentities; but that together with their nothingness they have also a very perilous element we have a proof before us.

For who was more exalted than this man? Did he not surpass the whole world in wealth? Had he not climbed to the very pinnacle of distinction? Did not all tremble and fear before him? Yet lo! He has become more wretched than the prisoner, more pitiable than the menial slave, more indigent than the beggar wasting away with hunger, having every day a vision of sharpened swords and of the criminal's grave, and the public executioner leading him out to his death; and he does not even know if he once enjoyed past pleasure, nor is he sensible even of the sun's ray, but at mid day his sight is dimmed as if he were encompassed by the densest gloom. But even let me try my best I shall not be able to present to you in language the suffering which he must naturally undergo, in the hourly expectation of death. But indeed what need is there of any words from me, when he himself has clearly depicted this for us as in a visible image? For yesterday when they came to him from the royal court intending to drag him away by force, and he ran for refuge to the holy furniture, his face was then, as it is now, no better than the countenance of one dead: and the chattering of his teeth, and the quaking and quivering of his whole body, and his faltering voice, and stammering tongue, and in fact his whole general appearance were suggestive of one whose soul was petrified.

Now I say these things not by way of reproaching him, or insulting his misfortune, but from a desire to soften your minds towards him, and to induce you to compassion, and to persuade you to be contented with the punishment which has already been inflicted. For since there are many inhuman persons among us who are inclined, perhaps, to find fault with me for having admitted him to the sanctuary, I parade his sufferings from a desire to soften their hardheartedness by my narrative.

For tell me, beloved brother, wherefore are you indignant with me? You say it is because he who continually made war upon the Church has taken refuge within it. Yet surely we ought in the highest degree to glorify God, for permitting him to be placed in such a great strait as to experience both the power and the lovingkindness of the Church:—her power in that he has suffered this great vicissitude in consequence of the attacks which he made upon her: her lovingkindness in that she whom he attacked now casts her shield in front of him and has received him under her wings, and placed him in all security not resenting any of her former injuries, but most lovingly opening her bosom to him.

For this is more glorious than any kind of trophy, this is a brilliant victory, this puts both Gentiles and Jews to shame, this displays the bright aspect of the Church: in that having received her enemy as a captive, she spares him, and when all have despised him in his desolation, she alone like an affectionate mother has concealed him under her cloak, opposing both the wrath of the king, and the rage of the people, and their overwhelming hatred. This is an ornament for the altar. A strange kind of ornament, you say, when the accused sinner, the extortioner, the robber is permitted to lay hold of the altar. Nay! say not so: for even the harlot took hold of the feet of Jesus, she who was stained with the most accursed and unclean sin: yet her deed was no reproach to Jesus, but rather redounded to His admiration and praise: for the impure woman did no injury to Him who was pure, but rather was the vile harlot rendered pure by the touch of Him who was the pure and spotless one.

Grudge not then, O man. We are the servants of the crucified one who said *Forgive them for they know not what they do*. But, you say, he cut off the right of refuge here by his ordinances and various kinds of laws. Yes! Yet now he has learned by experience what it was he did, and he himself by his own deeds has been the first to break the law, and has become a spectacle to the whole world, and silent though he is, he utters from thence a warning voice to all, saying do not such things as I have done, that you suffer not such things as I suffer. He appears as a teacher by means of his calamity, and the altar emits great lustre, inspiring now the greatest awe from the fact that it holds the lion in bondage;

for any figure of royalty might be very much set off if the king were not only to be seen seated on his throne arrayed in purple and wearing his crown, but if also prostrate at the feet of the king barbarians with their hands bound behind their backs were bending low their heads.

And that no persuasive arguments have been used, you yourselves are witnesses of the enthusiasm, and the concourse of the people. For brilliant indeed is the scene before us to day, and magnificent the assembly, and I see as large a gathering here today as at the Holy Paschal Feast. Thus the man has summoned you here without speaking and yet uttering a voice through his actions clearer than the sound of a trumpet: and you have all thronged hither today, maidens deserting their boudoirs, and matrons the women's chambers, and men the market place that you may see human nature convicted, and the instability of worldly affairs exposed, and the harlot-face which a few days ago was radiant (such is the prosperity derived from extortion) looking uglier than any wrinkled old woman, this face I say you may see denuded of its enamel and pigments by the action of adversity as by a sponge.

Such is the force of this calamity: it has made one who was illustrious and conspicuous appear the most insignificant of men. And if a rich man should enter the assembly he derives much profit from the sight: for when he beholds the man who was shaking the whole world, now dragged down from so high a pinnacle of power, cowering with fright, more terrified than a hare or a frog, nailed fast to yonder pillar, without bonds, his fear serving instead of a

chain, panic-stricken and trembling, he abates his haughti-
ness, he puts down his pride, and having acquired the kind
of wisdom concerning human affairs which it concerns
him to have he departs instructed by example in the lesson
which Holy Scripture teaches by precept:—*All flesh is grass
and all the glory of man as the flower of grass: the grass withers
and the flower fails* or *They shall wither away quickly as the
grass, and as the green herb shall they quickly fail* or *like smoke
are his days,*[2] and all passages of that kind.

Again the poor man when he has entered and gazed at
this spectacle does not think meanly of himself, nor bewail
himself on account of his poverty, but feels grateful to his
poverty, because it is a place of refuge to him, and a calm
haven, and secure bulwark; and when he sees these things
he would many times rather remain where he is, than enjoy
the possession of all men for a little time and afterwards be
in jeopardy of his own life. Do you see how the rich and
poor, high and low, bond and free have derived no small
profit from this man's taking refuge here? Do you see how
each man will depart hence with a remedy, being cured
merely by this sight?

Well! Have I softened your passion, and expelled your
wrath? Have I extinguished your cruelty? Have I induced
you to be pitiful? Indeed I think I have; and your counte-
nances and the streams of tears you shed are proofs of it.
Since then your hard rock has turned into deep and fertile
soil let us hasten to produce some fruit of mercy, and to

---

[2] See Is 40:6-7; Ps 37:2; and Js 4:14.

display a luxuriant crop of pity by falling down before the
Emperor or rather by imploring the merciful God so to
soften the rage of the Emperor, and make his heart tender
that he may grant the whole of the favour which we ask. For
indeed already since that day when this man fled here for
refuge no slight change has taken place; for as soon as the
Emperor knew that he had hurried to this asylum, although
the army was present, and incensed on account of his misdeeds, and demanded him to be given up for execution, the
Emperor made a long speech endeavouring to allay the
rage of the soldiers, maintaining that not only his offenses,
but any good deed which he might have done ought to be
taken into account, declaring that he felt gratitude for the
latter, and was prepared to forgive him as a fellow creature for deeds which were otherwise. And when they again
urged him to avenge the insult done to the imperial majesty,
shouting, leaping, and brandishing their spears, he shed
streams of tears from his gentle eyes, and having reminded
them of the Holy Table to which the man had fled for refuge he succeeded at last in appeasing their wrath.

Moreover let me add some arguments which concern ourselves. For what pardon could you deserve, if the
Emperor bears no resentment when he has been insulted,
but you who have experienced nothing of this kind display
so much wrath? And how after this assembly has been dissolved will you handle the holy mysteries, and repeat that
prayer by which we are commanded to say forgive us as we
also forgive our debtors when you are demanding vengeance
upon your debtor? Has he inflicted great wrongs and insults

on you? I will not deny it. Yet this is the season not for
judgment but for mercy; not for requiring an account, but
for showing loving kindness: not for investigating claims
but for conceding them; not for verdicts and vengeance, but
for mercy and favour. Let no one then be irritated or vexed,
but let us rather beseech the merciful God to grant him a
respite from death, and to rescue him from this impending
destruction, so that he may put off his transgression, and let
us unite to approach the merciful Emperor beseeching him
for the sake of the Church, for the sake of the altar, to con-
cede the life of one man as an offering to the Holy Table.

If we do this the Emperor himself will accept us, and
even before his praise we shall have the approval of God,
who will bestow a large recompense upon us for our mercy.
For as He rejects and hates the cruel and inhuman, so does
He welcome and love the merciful and humane man; and
if such a man be righteous, all the more glorious is the
crown which is wreathed for him: and if he be a sinner, He
passes over his sins granting this as the reward of compassion shown to his fellow-servant. For He says, *I will have
mercy and not sacrifice*, and throughout the Scriptures you
find Him always enquiring after this, and declaring it to be
the means of release from sin.

Thus, then, we shall dispose Him to be propitious to
us, thus we shall release ourselves from our sins, thus we
shall adorn the Church, thus also our merciful Emperor,
as I have already said, will commend us, and all the people will applaud us, and the ends of the earth will admire
the humanity and gentleness of our city, and all who hear

of these deeds throughout the world will extol us. That we then may enjoy these good things, let us fall down in prayer and supplication, let us rescue the captive, the fugitive, the suppliant from danger that we ourselves may obtain the future blessings by the favour and mercy of our Lord Jesus Christ, to whom be glory and power, now and for ever, world without end. Amen.

Saint Augustine of Hippo

AGAINST THE PAGANS

It makes a difference what you believe,
what you hope for, what you love.

BECAUSE HIS CHRISTIAN example looms so large in history and overshadows almost everything else from his culture, we might forget that Saint Augustine of Hippo lived and ministered in a world still largely pagan. Living side by side with those who worshipped false gods, Christians experienced the temptation to compromise their faith so as to fit in with the dominant culture. Recognizing the danger, Augustine labored to confirm his people in their identity as children of God, distinct from the pagans around them. On the calends of January in 404, he preached a long sermon to his people while celebrations for the new year raged outside. As in our own culture, calends (New Year's) was a time of widespread indulgence and immorality. But in

Augustine's day, this immorality was explicitly combined with pagan worship. In this excerpt from the much longer work, Augustine describes what it means to be, in Saint Paul's words, "children of God without blemish in the midst of a crooked and perverse generation" (Phil 2:15).

DISCOURSE AGAINST THE PAGANS

I WOULD URGE your graces, since I observe that you have come together here today as if it were a feast, and have gathered for this particular day in greater numbers than usual, to fix most firmly in your memories what you sang just now. Don't let it be a case of noisy tongues and dumb minds; rather, what your voices have been shouting in one another's ears, let your feelings cry out in the ears of God. This, after all, is what you were singing: *Save us, Lord our God, and gather us from among the nations, that we may confess your holy name* (Ps 106:47).[3]

And now, if the festival of the nations which is taking place today in the joys of the world and the flesh, with the din of silly and disgraceful songs, with the celebration of this false feast day—if the things the Gentiles are doing

---

[3] When St. Augustine writes "from among the nations," he seems to mean something like, "from the Gentiles" or "from the pagans." See Augustine, "Exposition on Psalm 106." *Nicene and Post-Nicene Fathers, First Series*, Vol. 8. Edited by Philip Schaff. Buffalo, NY: Christian Literature Publishing Co. 1888.

today do not meet with your approval, you will be gathered from among the nations.

You were certainly singing—and the sound of the divine song must still be echoing in your ears—*Save us, Lord our God, and gather us from among the nations.* Can you be gathered from among the nations without being saved, made safe and sound? So those who mix with the nations are not safe and sound, while those who are gathered from among the nations are made safe with the soundness of faith, a spiritual soundness, the soundness of the promises of God, the soundness of a good hope, the soundness of the most genuine charity.

So if you believe, hope, and love, it doesn't mean that you are immediately to be declared safe and sound and saved. It makes a difference, you see, what you believe, what you hope for, what you love. Nobody in fact can live any style of life without those three sentiments of the soul, of believing, hoping, loving. If you don't believe what the nations believe, and don't hope for what the nations hope for, and don't love what the nations love, then you are gathered from among the nations. And don't let your being physically mixed up with them alarm you, when there is such a wide separation of minds. What after all could be so widely separated as that they believe demons are gods, you on the other hand believe in the God who is the true God? That they hope for the vanities of this age, you hope for eternal life? That they love the world, you love the world's architect?

So if you believe something different from them, hope for something different, love something different, you should prove it by your life, demonstrate it by your actions. Are you going to join today in the celebration of good luck presents with a pagan, going to play at dice with a pagan, going to get drunk with a pagan? How in that case are you really believing something different, hoping for something different, loving something different? How can you keep your countenance as you sing *Save us, Lord our God, and gather us from among the nations.* You're segregated from the nations, after all, when you mix physically with the nations, but differ in your style of life. And you can see how wide apart this segregation sets you, if only you act accordingly to prove it.

It's like this: our Lord Jesus Christ, the Son of God, who became man for us, has already paid the price for us. And so if he has already paid the price, the reason he paid it was to redeem us, to gather us from among the nations. But if you get mixed up with the nations, it means you don't want to follow the one who redeemed you. Instead, you are mixing with them in lifestyle, actions, mind and heart by hoping for such things, believing such things, loving such things. You are being ungrateful to your Redeemer, you are not acknowledging the price paid for you, the blood of the Lamb without blemish. So in order to follow your Redeemer, who redeemed you with his blood, don't mix with the nations by the same kind of morals and actions. They give good luck presents; see to it that you give alms (Lk 11:41).

You see, I'm not telling you, brothers and sisters, "They give, don't you go giving"; on the contrary, give more than they do, but like people who believe something different, hope for something different, love something different. Because I'm not telling you, "They believe, don't you believe; they hope, don't you hope; they love, don't you love." Rather I'm telling you, "They believe that; as for you, believe this. They hope for that; as for you, hope for this. They love that; as for you, love this. They give that sort of thing, or to that sort of person; as for you, give this sort of thing or to this sort of person." So then, they give good luck presents; as for you, give alms. They entertain themselves with lascivious songs; as for you, entertain yourselves with the words of the scriptures. They run off to the theater, you people to church; they are getting drunk; you see to it that you fast. If you do all this, you have genuinely sung *Save us, Lord our God, and gather us from among the nations.*

At this moment, of course, those who are happy to hear what I have been saying are standing all together with those who are not so happy to hear it; and yet the former have already been gathered from among the nations, the latter are still mixed in with the nations. I am now speaking to real Christians; if you believe what the nations, the Gentiles, believe, if you hope for what the Gentiles hope for, if you love what the Gentiles love, then by all means live as the Gentiles live. But if you believe something else, hope for something else, love something else, then live in another kind of way, and prove how vastly different your faith and hope and charity are by the vast difference of your morals.

So if you have all come to life again with the heat of the charity of Christ, let your desire for him burn so brightly in your hearts, that no blast from those who would dissuade you from it can extinguish it. You see, I know perfectly well what you are going to have to endure when you leave here—and thank heaven that you have come together here at all. Because of course that you should assemble here during these days in greater numbers than usual doesn't displease me; on the contrary, it even gives me great pleasure. It means, after all, that because those who don't share your style of life are all hurrying off to occupy themselves with a variety of empty pleasures, and so are presenting you with time off and a holiday, you have found a way of bringing about in you what is said in the psalm: *Save us, Lord our God, and gather us from among the nations* (Ps 106:47).

So you have been gathered together right now; even if you go out and mix with them in general social intercourse, without however consenting to their bad and worthless ways, you will remain gathered from among the Gentiles, wherever you may actually be. And if only it were just in the streets that you have to put up with such shameless opposition, and not also, it may be, in your own homes! The father would like to fast, the son wouldn't, or the son would like to, the father wouldn't; or the husband wants to, the wife doesn't, or she does and he doesn't. So any who don't want to fast, and don't want to precisely because they regard this as a feast day, are a contrary head wind. The others, though, should burn so brightly that not only can they not be blown out themselves, but the opposition can also catch fire from them.

Just consider, my brothers and sisters, and take note
in sorrow. They [the pagans] have seen that they stand in
need of purgation, in order that that light, which cannot
be grasped by the mind's feeble gaze, may eventually be
grasped by the same gaze once it has been put into shape
and strengthened. They have seen that there is a need of
some medicine, and while they were looking around for
such a medicine the devil immediately presented himself, because they were looking around in pride, preening
themselves, as it were, on their own teachings; above all
because they were able, if anyone has been, to attain such
acuteness of wit and sharpness of mind, that transcending
all created things, both bodily and spiritual, they came to
understand that there is something which is both spiritual
and unchangeable, and that from it come all these things
that subsist in either a spiritual or a bodily mode. This, they
realized, makes it a kind of medium in the middle, because
God at the top is subject to motion neither in space nor in
time, while the substance of bodies, that is, the part of creation at the bottom, is subject to motion both in space and
in time. Hence that other substance is the medium in the
middle, because it is not subject to motion in space, as God
isn't either, while it is subject to motion in time, like bodies.

So while they were seeing the need for purgation and
searching for it, that proud being the devil stepped in and
accosted them as they were proudly seeking and proudly
preening themselves, and presented himself as a mediator,
through whom it seemed to them that their souls could be
purged.

But we have to ask what a mediator is. There is, you see, a false mediator, there is a true one. The false mediator, as I have often said, is the devil. He puts himself forward, by performing certain signs and wonders, to those who seek in a bad way and want something to pride themselves on.

But the true mediator, the Lord Jesus Christ, is one, and the humble men of old also acknowledged him through his revealing himself to them and wished to be purified through him. Before he was born of Mary he revealed himself to those who were worthy, so that they might be saved through faith in him who was going to be born and to suffer, just as we are saved through faith in him who has been born and has suffered. That indeed is why he came in such humble fashion, to show that he only purifies and saves the humble.

At that time, after all, before the Word had become flesh, it was not only among the Hebrew people to the holy patriarchs and prophets that he used to reveal himself; there are also in fact examples to be found in other nations, since the humble mediator never failed any people who sought him humbly, he the only one who reconciles to the Father, who alone could most truly say, "Nobody comes to the Father except through me" (Jn 14:6). He accommodated his humility to them, so that persevering in humility they might deserve to be purified through him, the humble mediator. Was Melchizedek, after all, of the people of Israel? And yet scripture commends him as priest of God Most High (Gn 14:18-19), as prefiguring the mediator himself. I mean, it is by him that even Abraham is blessed. Nobody, though, unless purified through the mediator, can come to that which cannot be obtained except by the most purified, even if it can be glimpsed in however small a degree by a certain intelligence of soul.

So then, even if some of them sought, as the apostle says, in such a way that they could descry the invisible things of God, understanding them through the things that were made (Rom 1:20), but in such a way too that they held onto the truth of God in a lie (Rom 1:18), that is, that they called themselves wise and were puffed up with pride, not worthily honoring him from whom they had received their understanding—to such as these, as I said, that proud mediator [the devil] presented himself as to the proud, just as the humble one [Christ] did to the humble, through certain matching suitabilities and through a certain inexpressible and wonderful justice, which abides in God's inner sanctum, and which we should respect even if we cannot see it. That proud mediator, therefore, comes to meet the proud, the humble one to meet the humble; but the reason the humble one comes to the humble is to lead them to the heights of God; the reason the proud one comes to the proud is to bar the heights of God to those who are high and mighty in themselves.

Sins bar the way; but mortality does not, because mortality is the punishment of sin, coming from the judgment of God. What bars the way is the thing that deserved this punishment. What I'm saying is this: it is not what God has done to you that bars your way to God, but what you have done to yourself. The mortality of the body, you see, is what God has done to you, while sin is what you have done to yourself. And so that true and trustworthy mediator has shared with you what God has done to you by way of retribution, but he has not shared with you what you have done to yourself by way of sin. He has shared mortality with you, but not shared iniquity with you.

He was made subject to death, you see, in the flesh, not however made through sin a debtor owing a death. For he emptied himself, taking the form of a slave, being made in the likeness of men, and being found in condition as a man (Phil 2:7). This was not said in such a way that we should conclude he had been changed, but because he wished to be manifested in a humble and servile guise, while remaining secretly Lord and God with God, the Son equal to the Father, through whom all things were made (Jn 1:3). And so having taken on mortality and shared with us the infirmity of our punishment, he purifies us from sins and sets us free from that very mortality, the reason he was found worthy to slay death by dying being that he suffered death without deserving it. This is the true and trustworthy mediator, the humble and exalted mediator, leading us back to where we had fallen from.

The reason the proud are more readily led astray by the proud mediator is that the proud are offended more by mortality than by iniquity, and that is why they are quicker to abhor mortality in Christ's humanity than iniquity in the devil's pride. And so he leads them, bloated as they are with vain and false doctrines. He has the audacity to boast that he is stronger and mightier than Christ because he was not born of a woman in the flesh, not arrested, not scourged, not spattered with spittle, not crowned with thorns, not hung on a cross, not dead and buried.

These are all things that the proud deride, which the humble mediator underwent, not taking upon himself iniquity with men and women and taking upon himself humanity, in order to heal them of the tumor of pride and make them conquerors of that false mediator, when they have learned to confess their sins, and have been purified through the justice of Christ from their own injustice, and have come through lowly fellowship with his mortality to the sublime summit of immortality.

And so, brothers and sisters, let us spurn the malign mediator, the self-deceiving and deceitful mediator, the mediator who does not reconcile but separates more and more. Let no one promise you any kind of purification out-side the Church, whether in temples or anywhere else, by means of sacrilegious sacred rites.

Let no one turn you away from God, no one from the Church; no one from God your Father, no one from the Church your mother. We had two parents who gave birth to us for mortality, we have two who give birth to us for immortality, God and the Church. Those gave birth to heirs to succeed them, these give birth to heirs to abide with them. Why else, after all, are we born of human parents, except in order to succeed them when they are dead? But we are brought forth by our Father, God, and our mother, the Church, in such a way as to live with our parents for-ever. Any who go off to sacrilegious rites or magical arts, or go consulting astrologers, augurs, diviners about their life

or anything to do with this life, have cut themselves off
from their Father, even if they do not leave the Church.
If any, though, have cut themselves off from the Church
by the division of schism, even though they may seem to
themselves to be holding on to the Father, they are most
perniciously forsaking their mother, while those who relin-
quish both Christian faith and mother Church are deserting both parents. Hold on to your Father, hold on to your
mother. You are a little child; stick to your mother. You are a
little child; suck your mother's milk, and she will bring you,
nourished on milk, to the table of the Father.

Your savior took flesh to himself, your mediator took
flesh to himself, and by taking flesh he took the Church
to himself. He was the first to make a libation, as coming
from the head, of what he would offer to God, a high priest
for ever (Heb 5:6), and the propitiation for our sins (1 Jn
2:2). The Word took human nature to himself, and the two
became one, as it is written, "They shall be two in one flesh.
This is a great sacrament, he says, but I mean in Christ and
in the Church" (Eph 5:31–32). The bridal chamber of this
marriage was the womb of the virgin. "And he, like a bride-
groom coming forth from his chamber, exulted like a giant
to run the way" (Ps 19:5). A giant because strong, overcom-
ing weakness with weakness, annihilating death with death.

But he ran on the way; he did not stop on the way, in
order not to become the man who was signified as having
stopped on the way of sinners. For when the psalm says,
"Blessed the one who has not turned aside in the counsel of
the ungodly, and has not stopped on the way of sinners" (Ps

1:1), it signifies a particular man who did stop on the way of sinners. So the Lord Jesus Christ ran on the way of sinners, but Adam stopped on the way of sinners. And because he stopped, he was wounded by robbers, he fell and lay there. But the one who was traveling along this way, not stopping but running, saw him; he found him wounded, put him on his beast, and handed him over to the innkeeper, because he himself was running the way in order to fulfill what had been foretold about him: "He drinks from the torrent on the way; therefore he shall lift up the head" (Ps 110:7). The torrent, you see, is this world. Waters which flow as a result of sudden storms or winter floods are called torrents—which are, of course, going to stop flowing just as quickly. That's what all these affairs of time are like—a transient torrent, soon going to cease.

Today, New Year's Day, those who are enjoying the excesses and vanities of the world don't see that they are being swept along by the rushing force of the torrent. Let them summon back, if they can, this same day last year; let them at least call back yesterday. They don't see that their enjoyments too pass like a torrent, so that they will find themselves saying later on.

And the reason why, for the sake of the purification that is effected by a mediator, the one who is equal to the Father wished to be the one mediator and himself become man was so that we through a related substance (because he is man) might attain to the supreme substance (because he is God). And the reason he descended was because we were in the lower regions, while he ascended so that we might not remain in the lower regions. He is the one true mediator who cheats nobody, who even while he is equal to the Father was also willing for our sakes to become less than he, not by losing what makes him equal, but by taking on what makes him less. He has already liberated even our flesh in his flesh. He dies now no more, and death will not lord it over him any further (Rom 6:9). It is to him that our prayers come, although in the liturgy of the Church they are addressed to the Father.

He dies now no more. It is he, you see, the high priest, who offers them, having offered himself as a holocaust for us. He is the one who takes us through to the end, confronting us on the way, not to block our way, but to direct it, not to separate, but to reconcile us, not to put obstacles in our way, but to break up all obstacles. He is the one and only pontiff, the one and only priest, who was prefigured in God's priests of old. That is why they used to look for a priest without bodily blemish, because he alone ever lived without the blemish of sin, even in his mortal body. For what was prefigured in their bodies found its real meaning in his life.

And so then, brothers and sisters, take real trouble over not sinning, exert yourselves energetically not to sin. But if anyone does sin, that one will purge our guilt who is the atonement for our sins (Jn 2:2). Avoid all those evil kinds of behavior for which God's name is blasphemed (Rom 2:24), so that your good manner of life may redound, by gaining others, to the glory of the name of Christ. Avoid those things which above all can separate you from God's altar.

As for the sins, though, which creep in every day through the habits of daily life, and never stop seeping in, as from the waves of the sea of this world, through whatever weaknesses we have, pump out the bilges with good works, to save the ship from being wrecked. Let these daily wounds be healed by the daily remedies of alms, fasting, prayers.

Be fervent in good works, neither showing off to men, for your own glory, what you do, nor avoiding the eyes of those who would like to imitate you, that they may see your good works, and glorify your Father who is in heaven (Mt 5:16). Whatever you do (Col 3:17), do all things for the glory of God (1 Cor 10:31), so that that humble and exalted one may exalt us from our humility. Our alms, you see, will reach him, who for our sakes became poor, though he was rich (2 Cor 8:9), in the same way as our fasting will reach him, who fasted for our sakes; in the same way too our prayers will reach him, when we sincerely ask in them that our debts may be forgiven, just as we too forgive our debtors (Mt 6:12), just as he too forgave his debtors, as he hung on the cross, saying, "Father, forgive them, because they do not know what they are doing" (Lk 23:34). Let that one be blessed, who gave you the ability to do whatever good you do do. Because if you attribute your good works to yourselves, and arrogate the credit to yourselves, so that you are being puffed up with pride in the very sacrifices of humility, you will be giving that false mediator his chance, enabling him to intrude himself and block your way.

Certainly you can see, brothers and sisters, to return now to what I was saying against the pagans, how you

should arm yourselves, not only so that you are not overcome by them, but also, insofar as this is within your com-
petence, that you may convince them and gain them for
salvation; and how you should pray and fast for them, that
they may come to know God and honor him as he should
be honored, not as the apostle says about some of them,
"because while they knew God, they did not glorify him as
God or give thanks, but they became futile in their thinking, and their senseless minds were darkened" (Rom 1:21),
so that they went looking for a superstitious and sacrilegious defilement under the name of purification. Wishing
to adhere, you see, to that thing which always is, which is
always the same, abiding unchangeable, they were able to
attain to it after a fashion by the acuteness of their wits, but
refused to honor it with humble hearts. So they stumbled
on that false mediator who is jealous of the human soul, and
strives by all available means to prevent it passing from the
labors and difficulties which he is in control of to that peace
where there is one more sublime than he is himself.

They can see the home country, as it were, from the
mountain of pride, from the mountain on the other side of
the valley. But nobody can go up to it without first coming
down. They refuse to come down so that they can go up;
that is, they refuse to be humble so that they can become
Christians.

Because the reason he was willing to become man was
to teach humility as God who had become man, not by
changing himself into a man, but by assuming a man, it
would seem that nothing could be added to such humility,

and yet in his human status he didn't choose the things on which human beings pride themselves. He didn't choose highborn parents, or ones of any professional distinction. I mean, it was his will to be born of a woman who was betrothed to a carpenter, so that nobody might boast of the rank of his parents as against the justice of someone poor and base-born, and so become incurably conceited.

Those people, you see, who as I was saying can see the home country from a long way off, and from the mountain of pride on the opposite side of the valley, scorn humility; that's why they don't stick to the way, because our way is humility. Christ showed us this way in himself. Any who deviate from this way will stumble upon a mountain of tangled and impenetrable thickets, the devil placing himself in their way, destructively and deceitfully intruding himself as a mediator through countless sacrilegious rites, through soothsayers, augurs, fortune-tellers, astrologers, magicians. People who are sold on these don't come down to the way, but wander around on a kind of wooded mountain, from which some of them lift up their eyes and see the home country, but they can't reach it, because they don't keep to the way.

Those on the other hand who do now keep to the way, that is, to the true and trustworthy mediator, the mediator who leads along the way and doesn't block it, the mediator who purges away guilt and doesn't involve us in it, these persevere in walking along in the faith they hold. Because some of them too can see the home country, some of them can't. But let those who can't yet see the home country not depart from the way, and they will reach exactly the same place as those who can.

So then, dearest brothers and sisters, don't let people scare you on this account either, when they say that these powers of the elements have to be placated and honored with their own sacraments on account of the necessities of life and the temporal goods that we need for our various uses, because in fact they have no power over these matters except what is allowed them from above. Recollect that that holy man Job could not even have been tested by such enormous trials, unless the tempter had received the power from the Lord God. And pay attention to what the apostle says: "God is faithful, who will not allow you to be tempted beyond what you can bear, but with the temptation he will also provide a way out, so that you may be able to endure" (1 Cor 10:13).

Also pay attention to those who do rely on such things, who bind up souls of light with the sacraments of demons and magical arts; observe how gratuitously they forfeit their salvation. They don't, after all, avoid suffering the same things as other people, or even suffering worse things with the torture of a bad conscience: financial losses, diseases, convictions, deaths, frequently sharing in the scourges common to the human race, frequently suffering too for their own misdeeds. Observe whether those who worship Neptune have better luck with their sea voyages than those who don't worship him; whether those who have bound themselves to the service of the temple of Tellus have richer harvests from their fields than those who have not tied themselves down to any such superstition; whether women who worship Juno give birth with slighter labor pains or less danger than Christian women who execrate her; whether those who worship Mercury are more quick-witted than those who pour scorn on such fancies, or else, because he is also said to be the god of commerce, whether those who sacrifice to him make bigger profits than those who refuse to contaminate themselves with any such sacrilege.

And in this way run the searching eye of your minds over all these temporal advantages; you will find that they are all controlled by the supreme authority of God. Christians who serve him alone and hold to his mediator, *the way* (Jn 14:6), care nothing for the deceptive enticements and terrors of such nonsense, but render honor to the most true God, whether their self-restraint is being tested by temporal prosperity, or their courage by temporal adversity, because *God is faithful, who does not allow us to be tempted beyond what we can bear, but with the temptation provides a way out, so that we may be able to endure* (1 Cor 10:13). Thus, he comforts us in all circumstances, and fills us with the joy of good hope (Wis 12:19), until he brings us through to the place we are being led to, by the way which he has in his gracious goodness provided for our weakness.

Pope Saint Leo the Great

ON THE ROLE OF PETER

Though He has delegated the care of His sheep to many shepherds, yet He has not Himself abandoned the guardianship of His beloved flock.

THE CHURCH'S FIRST eight centuries were characterized in large part by the Christological controversies: Was Jesus truly divine? Was he truly human? In the course of addressing these issues, another essential aspect of the Church emerged. Namely, that Saint Peter's office continues in the ministry of the bishop of Rome, the pope. As Peter received the duty to strengthen his brothers (cf. Lk 22:32), so also the pope must confirm the faithful in the truth. It is his duty to hand down to the faithful their rightful inheritance; that is, the Catholic faith in its fullness.

The most famous recognition of the pope's role came at the Council of Chalcedon in 451. When the "Tome of Leo" was read, the Fathers cried out with one voice, "Peter has spoken through Leo!" Years before, however, on the occasion of his third anniversary of election, Leo had already reflected on how Peter continues to minister through the bishop of Rome.

❧   ❧   ❧

ON THE ROLE OF PETER

As OFTEN AS God's mercy deigns to bring round the day of His gifts to us, there is, dearly-beloved, just and reasonable cause for rejoicing, if only our appointment to the office be referred to the praise of Him who gave it. For though this recognition of God may well be found in all His priests, yet I take it to be peculiarly binding on me, who, regarding my own utter insignificance and the greatness of the office undertaken, ought myself also to utter that exclamation of the Prophet: Lord, I heard Your speech and was afraid: I considered Your works and was dismayed. For what is so unwonted and so dismaying as labour to the frail, exaltation to the humble, dignity to the undeserving? And yet we do not despair nor lose heart, because we put our trust not in ourselves but in Him who works in us. And hence also we have sung with harmonious voice the psalm of David, dearly beloved, not in our own praise, but to the glory of Christ the Lord. For it is He of whom it is prophetically written, You are a priest for ever after the order of Melchizedeck, that is, not after the order of Aaron, whose priesthood descending along his own line of offspring was a temporal ministry, and ceased with the law of the Old Testament, but after the order of Melchizedeck, in whom was prefigured the eternal High Priest. And no reference is made to his parentage because in him it is understood that He was portrayed, whose generation cannot be declared. And finally, now that the mystery of this Divine priesthood has descended to human agency, it runs not by the line of birth, nor is that which flesh and blood created; chosen, but without regard to the privilege of paternity and succession by inheritance, those men are received by the Church as its rulers whom the Holy Ghost prepares: so that in the people of God's adoption, the whole body of which is priestly and royal, it is not the prerogative of earthly origin which obtains the unction, but the condescension of Divine grace which creates the bishop.

Although, therefore, dearly beloved, we be found both weak and slothful in fulfilling the duties of our office, because, whatever devoted and vigorous action we desire to do, we are hindered by the frailty of our very condition; yet having the unceasing propitiation of the Almighty and perpetual Priest, who being like us and yet equal with the Father, brought down His Godhead even to things human, and raised His Manhood even to things Divine, we worthily and piously rejoice over His dispensation, whereby, though He has delegated the care of His sheep to many shepherds, yet He has not Himself abandoned the guardianship of His beloved flock. And from His overruling and eternal protection we have received the support of the Apostles' aid also, which assuredly does not cease from its operation; and the strength of the foundation, on which the whole superstructure of the Church is reared, is not weakened by the weight of the temple that rests upon it. For the solidity of that faith which was praised in the chief of the Apostles is perpetual: and as that remains which Peter believed in Christ, so that remains which Christ instituted in Peter. For when, as has been read in the Gospel lesson, the Lord had asked the disciples whom they believed Him to be amid the various opinions that were held, and the blessed Peter had replied, saying, "You are the Christ, the Son of the living God", the Lord says:

> Blessed are you, Simon Bar-Jona, because flesh and
> blood has not revealed it to you, but My Father, which
> is in heaven. And I say to you, that you are Peter, and
> upon this rock will I build My church, and the gates
> of Hades shall not prevail against it. And I will give
> unto you the keys of the kingdom of heaven. And
> whatsoever you shall bind on earth, shall be bound in
> heaven; and whatsoever you shall loose on earth, shall
> be loosed also in heaven (Mt 16:16–19).

The dispensation of Truth therefore abides, and the blessed Peter persevering in the strength of the Rock, which he has received, has not abandoned the helm of the Church, which he undertook. For he was ordained before the rest in such a way that from his being called the Rock, from his being pronounced the Foundation, from his being constituted the Doorkeeper of the kingdom of heaven, from his being set as the Umpire to bind and to loose, whose judgments shall retain their validity in heaven, from all these mystical titles we might know the nature of his association with Christ. And still today he more fully and effectually performs what is entrusted to him, and carries out every part of his duty and charge in Him and with Him, through Whom he has been glorified. And so if anything is rightly done and rightly decreed by us, if anything is won from the mercy of God by our daily supplications, it is of his work and merits whose power lives and whose authority prevails in his See. For this, dearly-beloved, was gained by that confession, which, inspired in the Apostle's heart by God the Father, transcended all the uncertainty of human opinions, and was endued with the firmness of a rock, which no assaults could shake. For throughout the Church Peter daily says, *You are the Christ, the Son of the living God*, and every tongue which confesses the Lord, accepts the instruction his voice conveys. This Faith conquers the devil and breaks the bonds of his prisoners. It uproots us from this earth and plants us in heaven, and the gates of Hades cannot prevail against it. For with such solidity is it endued by God that the depravity of heretics cannot mar it nor the unbelief of the heathen overcome it.

And so, dearly beloved, with reasonable obedience we celebrate today's festival by such methods, that in my humble person he may be recognized and honoured, in whom abides the care of all the shepherds, together with the charge of the sheep commended to him, and whose dignity is not abated even in so unworthy an heir. And hence the presence of my venerable brothers and fellow priests, so much desired and valued by me, will be the more sacred and precious, if they will transfer the chief honour of this service in which they have deigned to take part to him whom they know to be not only the patron of this see, but also the primate of all bishops. When therefore we utter our exhortations in your ears, holy brethren, believe that he is speaking whose representative we are: because it is his warning that we give, nothing else but his teaching that we preach, beseeching you to gird up the loins of your mind (1 Pt 1:13), and lead a chaste and sober life in the fear of God, and not to let your mind forget his supremacy and consent to the lusts of the flesh. Short and fleeting are the joys of this world's pleasures which endeavour to turn aside from the path of life those who are called to eternity. The faithful and religious spirit, therefore, must desire the things which are heavenly, and being eager for the Divine promises, lift itself to the love of the incorruptible Good and the hope of the true Light. But be sure, dearly-beloved, that your labour, whereby you resist vices and fight against carnal desires, is pleasing and precious in God's sight, and in God's mercy will profit not only yourselves but me also, because the zealous pastor makes his boast of the progress of the Lord's flock. For you are my crown and joy (1 Thess 2:20), as the Apostle says; if your faith, which from the beginning of the Gospel has been preached in all the world has continued in love and holiness. For though the whole Church, which is in all the world, ought to abound in all virtues, yet you especially, above all people, it becomes to excel in deeds of piety, because founded as you are on the very citadel of the Apostolic Rock, not only has our Lord Jesus Christ redeemed you in common with all men, but the blessed Apostle Peter has instructed you far beyond all men. Through the same Christ our Lord.

Saint Charles Borromeo

TO SUPERIORS OF MONASTERIES AND OTHER RELIGIOUS PRIESTS

Will you risk your life for your flock?

WHEN CARDINAL BORROMEO entered his home Archdiocese of Milan in 1565, that city had been without a resident archbishop for eighty years. The arrival of the renowned reformer did not sit well with a clergy accustomed to living without governance or accountability. Nevertheless, Borromeo began his project of reform by frequent preaching and careful administration, two things unknown to the city for decades. His ministry during the plague of 1576 won Milan's affection most of all. The sight of him moving among the dying, risking his life to bring the sacraments into places of death, gave even more power to his sermons. His ministry and life demonstrate how the preacher's words strike deeper when preceded, accompanied, and followed by works of charity.

Hoping to prevail upon religious superiors for their assistance during the plague, he preached the following sermon to the superiors of monasteries and other religious priests.

WILL YOU RISK YOUR LIFE FOR THE FLOCK?

Sermon to superiors of monasteries and other religious priests at the time of the plague, 1576

W ERE I TO try and explain to you, brothers, the miserable and mournful condition of our city, I could only do it poorly. For there is no one who does not have such great miseries constantly before his eyes. Moreover, I do not consider anyone so hardhearted as not to be shattered in soul with pity [when he sees] people bereft of the presence of their most beloved heads of the city and of all help, pushed out of their own sweet familiar homes, sick and only half-alive, with all their goods left behind; and finally led on deathly, sordid carts to those enclosed areas which are much more like stables than civilized dwellings, and from which there is little or no hope of ever returning. In short, they are as if tightly held in the jaws of death.

These things are utterly miserable for human weakness to bear, but since they nevertheless concern time and this life only, they can appear tolerable, especially if someone is lifted up with hope for the life to come. But what shall we say about being deprived of those most helpful good things which lead above all to the happiness of the next life and eternal goods, and which, if someone loses them now, he also risks losing the good things which are to come and remain forever? That is most miserable, indeed grave and dangerous, both for those who suffer and for us, to whom the care and power of these things has been divinely given.

We know and see that as the body is wasting away by pestilence, so the devout souls of our brethren languish with desire for divine things. With voices only half-living, or by a gesture only, they request the Sacraments and implore mercy, but we with hard hearts delay or look away. As you know, we have kept the parish pastors in their post, but they are not enough for the multitude, as we know, unless each of them had the strength of many. In general, those who are led off to the quarantined houses are too far away to be helped by their own parish pastors. Not to mention the fact that parish pastors are often turned away by their subjects, if they have already ministered to the afflicted, until the passage of time can show that they themselves are healthy. And so it happens that even the residents of that priest's neighborhood need the service of other priests. I have sought outside priests, and not in vain, but we still need more, for the multitude of people led off to quarantine still lies helpless.

I do not find other priests willing to help, and I cannot force them, nor should I. I have recourse to you, whose condition and state in life manifests a disdain for all human things so that you aim exclusively at the worship of God and concern for the salvation of men. If there is anyone whom we could expect to come and save others and imitate the Lord in this way, it would be you first of all. I will certainly say that the sick do not need our assistance in such a way that without it they would have no hope of salvation, but often our services are necessary. Besides, it is indisputably clear that we all understand how much they benefit—not only the bad but also the good—and how much alleviation they usually bring to the sick body and above all to the soul solicitous for its salvation.

But how can those upon whom mercy has been given and liberally poured out be so tightly limited with theirs, and measure it out in accord with temporal and external necessities? The same Son of God, who for the sake of the salvation of all men, including his enemies and the impious, was fixed to the cross and died in the greatest shame and the bitterest torment, invites us to go forward into the danger of a quiet and glorious death for devout brethren. He to whom we owe as much repayment as we could not obtain by dying a thousand times without end, does not even request this pathetic life of ours, but only that we put it at risk. We see many go through these dangers without escaping death. Moreover, we even see many who are free from fear but still die. But if we do not escape it, this will not be death; rather it will be a quicker attainment of blessed glory, which is true life. For what does our poor life find in human things so as to be grateful for them instead of the most precious and immortal benefits of God should we lose this opportunity?

And why do we spare our life which in spite of everything we must lose after a few years, or days, or indeed hours, as the human condition dictates?

It is rather the case that with this disaster of our city, the danger and risk which charity toward our brethren may not demand, will inexorably be required of us by the contagion. Just like almost countless others, who nevertheless looked out for themselves with all diligence, we are going to die. How much more beautiful it is in this affair, if we anticipate what is necessary in any case and provide a victim most pleasing to God for our sins and for everything we owe to his immense goodness and majesty? Alas! We daily see many who undertake these same dangers, led on by the hope of some utterly meager reward which indeed they often do not obtain. Are we going to delay, though we have such good reasons and such great rewards offered to us?

Look to the law of obedience, by the strength of which you rightly wish your actions to be fortified in view of your salvation. I know you are not unaware that the Supreme Pontiff, common father and bishop of all, placed that in our hand. You also heard the reading of his letter, in which he vehemently exhorts us to this glorious and holy ministry of aiding the brethren. In that regard there is no question for anyone of looking to the will of the bishop or fearing his interdict, when it is the first one among all the bishops who both declared it to be his will and added his own exhortations.

I wish, brothers, for you to show this service to God, which, as I hope, you will accept. But you will also affect us with this very great benefit, which no forgetfulness shall ever wipe away. If my very great worry and sorrow is alleviated by your virtue, when I see some of you here ready to go ahead and offer your life to God and to me in this blessed test for the sake of this most holy work, then I do not doubt that with the open entrance into these ranks of several or even only a few of you, many others who are now terrified and, as it were, paralyzed by their apprehension of something so unusual, will follow the joyful example of going in the way now opened wide. Therefore, the man who goes first offers himself as an authority and a guide for others, and will greatly increase the weight of his merit.

Nor do I present you with any real ardor of charity. Our Fathers, incited by the spirit of God, did the same in similar circumstances. They taught that this is what should be done, as one can see clearly enough in the writings of the ancients collected and edited by our command. Moreover, they extolled a work of this kind because it has the greatest power to motivate our souls to confirm that they are the stuff of martyrs.

It is indeed a desirable time now when without the cruelty of the tyrant, without the rack, without fire, without beasts, and in the complete absence of harsh tortures which are usually the most frightful to human weakness, we can obtain the crown of martyrdom. What is even more, we can do so without the terrible hardship which always tends to accompany a disease of this type, in which the sick are everyone and given no support or help from anyone. What we shall give to any sick man, we certainly shall not deny to the father of the sick, and it will be to our benefit when the example we have given is imitated by others. Anyone can hope that he will come out safe, and all the more so than almost innumerable others whom we see continuously going about their business in the middle of this raging pestilence with no precautions and no self-control. But if someone does contract the disease, and others are no longer there, then I myself, who will be going about among you every day on account of the sick, will be there. I shall be charged with caring for your health in both body and soul. I will willingly come to your aid. I offer myself indeed on divine help, I have decided to spare no labors or dangers in order to fulfill my pastoral office and to serve the flock committed to me in any way I can for their salvation.

Saint Edmund Campion

CHALLENGE TO THE PRIVY COUNCIL (CAMPION'S BRAG)

*That which otherwise you must have sought for by practice
of wit, I do now lay into your hands by plain confession.*

WHILE A YOUNG Protestant at Oxford, Edmund Campion became known for his intelligence and eloquence, winning the esteem of Queen Elizabeth and her advisors. He then embarked on what could have been a distinguished—and safe—career in the Church of England. Not long after, however, he returned to the faith of his fathers and entered the Jesuits. He was ordained a priest and sent to minister to Catholics covertly in England, where in 1581 he was captured, hanged, drawn, and quartered.

"Campion's Brag" (as it was disparagingly called by adversaries) is not a sermon for the simple reason that no priest could preach publicly in Elizabethan England. His Challenge is a profession of faith, an explanation of his mission, and a request to defend the Faith openly. It presents Campion's style, theology, and spirit—and perhaps gives us a sense of how he would have preached if permitted.

❖ ❖ ❖

"CAMPION'S BRAG"

To the Right Honourable, the Lords of Her Majesty's Privy Council:

Whereas I have come out of Germany and Bohemia, being sent by my superiors, and adventured myself into this noble realm, my dear country, for the glory of God and benefit of souls, I thought it like enough that, in this busy, watchful, and suspicious world, I should either sooner or later be intercepted and stopped of my course.

Wherefore, providing for all events, and uncertain what may become of me, when God shall haply deliver my body into durance, I supposed it needful to put this in writing in a readiness, desiring your good lordships to give it your reading, for to know my cause. This doing, I trust I shall ease you of some labour. For that which otherwise you must have sought for by practice of wit, I do now lay into your hands by plain confession. And to the intent that the whole matter may be conceived in order, and so the better both understood and remembered, I make thereof these nine points or articles, directly, truly and resolutely opening my full enterprise and purpose.

1. I confess that I am (albeit unworthy) a priest of the

Catholic Church, and through the great mercy of God vowed now these eight years into the religion [religious order] of the Society of Jesus. Hereby I have taken upon me a special kind of warfare under the banner of obedience, and also resigned all my interest or possibility of wealth, honour, pleasure, and other worldly felicity.

II. At the voice of our General, which is to me a warrant from heaven and oracle of Christ, I took my voyage from Prague to Rome (where our General Father is always resident) and from Rome to England, as I might and would have done joyously into any part of Christendom or Heatheness, had I been thereto assigned.

III. My charge is, of free cost to preach the Gospel, to minister the Sacraments, to instruct the simple, to reform sinners, to confute errors—in brief, to cry alarm spiritual against foul vice and proud ignorance, wherewith many of my dear countrymen are abused.

IV. I never had mind, and am strictly forbidden by our Father that sent me, to deal in any respect with matter of state or policy of this realm, as things which appertain not to my vocation, and from which I gladly restrain and sequester my thoughts.

V. I do ask, to the glory of God, with all humility, and under your correction, three sorts of indifferent and quiet audiences: the first, before your Honours, wherein I will discourse of religion, so far as it toucheth the common weal and your nobilities: the second, whereof I make more account, before the Doctors and Masters and chosen men of both universities, wherein I undertake to avow the faith of our Catholic Church by proofs innumerable—Scriptures, councils, Fathers, history, natural and moral reasons: the third, before the lawyers, spiritual and temporal, wherein I will justify the said faith by the common wisdom of the laws standing yet in force and practice.

vi. I would be loath to speak anything that might sound of any insolent brag or challenge, especially being now as a dead man to this world and willing to put my head under every man's foot, and to kiss the ground they tread upon. Yet I have such courage in avouching the majesty of Jesus my King, and such affiance in his gracious favour, and such assurance in my quarrel, and my evidence so impregnable, and because I know perfectly that no one Protestant, nor all the Protestants living, nor any sect of our adversaries (howsoever they face men down in pulpits, and overrule us in their kingdom of grammarians and unlearned ears) can maintain their doctrine in disputation. I am to sue most humbly and instantly for combat with all and every of them, and the most principal that may be found: protesting that in this trial the better furnished they come, the better welcome they shall be.

vii. And because it hath pleased God to enrich the Queen my Sovereign Lady with notable gifts of nature, learning, and princely education, I do verily trust that if her Highness would vouchsafe her royal person and good attention to such a conference as, in the second part of my fifth article I have motioned, or to a few sermons, which in her or your hearing I am to utter such manifest and fair light by good method and plain dealing may be cast upon these controversies, that possibly her zeal of truth and love of her people shall incline her noble Grace to disfavour some proceedings hurtful to the realm, and procure towards us oppressed more equity.

VIII. Moreover I doubt not but you, her Highness' Council, being of such wisdom and discreet in cases most important, when you shall have heard these questions of religion opened faithfully, which many times by our adversaries are huddled up and confounded, will see upon what substantial grounds our Catholic Faith is builded, how feeble that side is which by sway of the time prevaileth against us, and so at last for your own souls, and for many thousand souls that depend upon your government, will discountenance error when it is bewrayed [revealed], and hearken to those who would spend the best blood in their bodies for your salvation. Many innocent hands are lifted up to heaven for you daily by those English students, whose posterity shall never die, which beyond seas, gathering virtue and sufficient knowledge for the purpose, are determined never to give you over, but either to win you heaven, or to die upon your pikes. And touching our Society, be it known to you that we have made a league—all the Jesuits in the world, whose succession and multitude must overreach all the practice of England—cheerfully to carry the cross you shall lay upon us, and never to despair your recovery, while we have a man left to enjoy your Tyburn, or to be racked with your torments, or consumed with your prisons. The expense is reckoned, the enterprise is begun; it is of God; it cannot be withstood. So the faith was planted: So it must be restored.

IX. If these my offers be refused, and my endeavours can take no place, and I, having run thousands of miles to do you good, shall be rewarded with rigour, I have no more to say but to recommend your case and mine to Almighty God, the Searcher of Hearts, who send us his grace, and see us at accord before the day of payment, to the end we may at last be friends in heaven, when all injuries shall be forgotten.

Jacques-Bénigne Bossuet

ON PREACHING THE GOSPEL

*Today I propose to prepare you worthily
to receive that immortal food.*

IN SOME WAYS, the greatest crisis of faith is the one that
is unfelt and unseen. It is the crisis of complacency that
often plagues Catholic cultures. Surrounded by other
Catholics and the trappings of Catholicism, the faithful
grow tepid and begin to take the Faith for granted. Without even noticing, they become unmoved and unmov-
able by the Gospel. Such was the danger for Catholics in
seventeenth-century France. The entire realm was Catholic,
and the Church enjoyed the patronage of the king. Catholics could—and many did—easily fall into a presumptuous
living of the Faith. It was in that milieu that Jacques-Bénigne Bossuet ministered and preached.

Although unknown to most English readers, Bossuet
is commonly regarded as the finest French orator. Coming

from wealth and privilege, he used his talents and training
to serve the Gospel and to combat the lukewarm Catholicism of his countrymen. He was renowned for his preaching and soon became a favorite of the royal court. This
sermon was the first in a series preached in Lent of 1662
before Louis XIV. Doubtlessly looking ahead to the other
sermons he would give, Bossuet brilliantly describes the
purposes of preaching, and in so doing, sounds a warning
against complacency.

❊   ❊   ❊

ON PREACHING THE GOSPEL[4]

THE VAST SILENCE of God amidst the disorder of man-
kind is astonishing. Day by day, his commandments
are forgotten, his truths blasphemed, and the prerogatives
of his rule transgressed, yet the sun shines upon the scoffers,
the rain waters their fields, and the earth is stable under
their feet. He sees all, and he acts as though he did not. He
considers all things and says nothing at all.

---

[4] "On Preaching the Gospel" was the sermon for the first Sunday of
Lent, preached by Jacques-Bénigne Bossuet before Louis XIV at
the Chapel of the Louvre on 26 February 1662. This translation by
Christopher O. Blum was made from the text in Bossuet's *Oeuvres
Oratoires*, édition critique de l'abbé J. Lebarq, revue et augmentée
par Ch. Urbain et E. Levesque (Paris: Desclée, 1926), IV: 172-92.
Unless otherwise noted, quotations from Sacred Scripture are from
the Revised Standard Version, Catholic Edition.

I am mistaken. He does speak. His goodness, his generosity, his very silence are so many voices inviting sinners to repentance. Yet as our hard hearts are deaf to these kinds of speech, he makes another voice resound, a voice that speaks with precision and authority, a voice that calls us to repent. He does not speak to judge us; he speaks to warn us, and it is this voice of warning that echoes in all our pulpits. This is the voice made known to us in our Gospel, a voice to serve as nourishment during our time of fasting and as a support for our weakness: "Not by bread alone does man live, but by every word that comes forth from the mouth of God" (Mt 4:4). Today I propose to prepare you worthily to receive that immortal food. But, O God, what use will my words be if you do not open hearts and dispose minds to welcome your Holy Spirit? Descend, then, O Divine Spirit and prepare your own way. And you, O most holy Virgin, lend us your charitable aid, so that the work of your beloved Son may be accomplished in our hearts. This we pray you humbly, in the words of the angel: *Ave Maria* . . .

Although Jesus Christ is the Lord of lords and the Prince of the kings of the earth, and although his reign is entirely free and sovereign, he wished nevertheless to give an example of moderation and justice to all kings who depend upon his power, and so he voluntarily subjected himself to the rules he had made and the laws he had established. In his Gospel, he ordained that gentle ways should precede rigorous ones, and that sinners should be warned before they are judged. He practiced what he prescribed, for "inasmuch", as the Apostle says, "as he has fixed a day on which he will judge the world in righteousness, he first calls upon all men everywhere to repent" (Acts 17:30-1). That is to say, before mounting his tribunal to condemn the guilty with a rigorous sentence, he first speaks in the pulpits, to draw them back to the narrow path by means of charitable warnings.

In this holy time of penance, we should pay special attention to this fatherly voice. For while it deserves profound respect at all times, and while listening to sacred discourses is always one of the most important duties of Christian piety, it has ever been a wise practice to consecrate a time especially for them, so that, if such be our blindness that we abandon almost the whole of our lives to vanity, there should be at least a few days during which we hear the truth that would counsel us charitably before our sentences are levied, and which comes to enlighten us before we are measured against it and brought low.

Come, then, O holy truth! Make known your accusation of our evil ways, light up this dark and shadowy age, shine in the eyes of the faithful, so that those who do not know you may hear you, those who do not think of you may look upon you, and those who do not love you may embrace you.

Here, in brief compass, are the three chief ends of the preaching of the Gospel. Men either do not know the truth, or they do not think about the truth, or they are not moved by the truth. When they do not know the truth, she speaks to them in order to enlighten their intellects, for she would not have them be deceived. When they do not think about the truth, she speaks to them to gain their attention, for she would not have them be taken by surprise. When they are not moved by the truth, she speaks to them to kindle their affections and to excite their languishing love for her, for she would not have them be condemned.

If I can today shed light upon these three important ends, the faithful will see clearly why they should be attentive to the preaching of the Gospel. If they are not well instructed, the Holy Spirit will dispel their ignorance. If they are sufficiently enlightened, he will prompt them to think about what they know. If they think without being moved, he will place in the depth of their hearts what had only been skimming on the surface of their minds. And as these three great effects contain the entire fruit of sacred discourses, I will also make them the subject and the division of this one, which will be, as you shall see, the necessary preparation and foundation for those which are to follow.

I

As the truth of God, our immutable law, has two different states, one which concerns the present age and another which looks to the world to come, one by which human life is ruled and another by which it is judged, so also does the Holy Spirit make the truth appear to us in the Scriptures under two different guises, and with qualities fitting to them both. In the 119th Psalm, where David speaks so capably of the law of God, he sometimes calls it by the name of commandment, sometimes that of counsel, and other times by the names of judgment or testimony. And while these four names signify nothing other than the law of God, it must all the same be noted that the first two are proper to the age in which we now live and that the others are more fitting to the one which we await.

In this present age, the truth of God that appears in his law is at once an absolute commandment and a charitable counsel. It is a commandment that embodies the will of a sovereign, and it is also the counsel by which we are offered the advice of a friend. It is a commandment because in it the sovereign prescribes what the interests of his service require of us. It is counsel because in it a friend shows us what a care for our salvation demands. The preachers of the Gospel declare the law of God in their pulpits according to these two qualities: as a commandment, insofar as it is necessary and indispensable, and as counsel insofar as it is useful and advantageous. If by the same crime we fail in what we owe to God and what we owe to ourselves, we thereby show our disdain for the orders of a sovereign as well as for the counsel of a friend. Then this same truth will, in time, take on another form, and will become a testimony that convicts us, and a final sentence that condemns us: "The word that I have spoken," said the Son of God, "will be his judge on the last day" (John 12:48). That is to say that excuses will not be heard, nor will amnesty be granted. The word, he says, will judge you: the law itself will make the sentence according to its proper tenor, in the extreme rigor of what is right; and from this we must understand that it will be a judgment without mercy.

Fear of this judgment, therefore, is what makes preachers ascend into the pulpit. One day, as St. Paul tells us, "we
must all appear before the judgment seat of Jesus Christ."
Thus, he continues, "knowing the fear of the Lord, we persuade men" (2 Cor 5:10–11). Knowing that this judgment
is certain, rigorous, and inevitable, we come early to prepare
you for it. We come to set before you the unchanging laws
by which your cause will be decided and to place in your
hands the articles on which you will be questioned, so that
you may begin to consider your responses while there is still
time.

Should you think that the holy truths are sufficiently
well known, and that the faithful do not need to be
instructed in them, then recall that God laments through
the mouth of his prophet Isaiah that not only infidels and
strangers, but "my people," yes, his own people, "go into
exile for want of knowledge" (Isaiah 5:13). And lest we
imagine that those who perish for want of knowledge are
the poor and uneducated, he declares in precise terms that
it is the powerful, the rich, the great, and even princes who
neglect to learn of their particular obligations as well as of
the common duties of piety, and who therefore fall into the
eternal abyss: "Sheol has enlarged its appetite and opened
its mouth beyond measure, and the nobility of Jerusalem
and her multitude go down" (Isaiah 5:14).

Not only do we often ignore the holy truths, we sometimes find our affections set entirely against them. The
thought may surprise you. Perhaps you will respond that
your heart does not rebel against the Faith and that you

do not listen to those doctors of the court who give public lessons of libertinism and support their dangerous opinions by well-crafted speeches. I praise your piety for such a necessary precaution. But do not persuade yourself that for this you are thereby exempt from error. For it must be understood that error can overcome us in two ways: sometimes it overflows like floodwaters and carries us away all at once; but sometimes it falls little by little and corrupts us drop by drop. What I mean is that sometimes a declared libertinism overturns the principles of religion by a single tremendous effort, and that sometimes a more hidden force, like that of the bad examples and practices of the world, saps its foundations by the insensible progress of many repeated blows. Thus you make no great progress if you refrain from swallowing the poison of libertinism all at once while you nevertheless sip it little by little, if you let it insensibly win your heart by the subtle contagion that one breathes in with the air of the conversations and customs of the fashionable world.

Who could here recount all the world's errors? That subtle, dangerous master holds public classes without dogmatizing. It has its particular method of not proving its maxims, but of impressing them upon us without our noticing them. As many are the men who speak to us, so many are the organs who breathe these maxims into us. Our enemies from malice and our friends from their good intentions share equally in giving us false ideas of good and evil. All that is said in the world recommends either ambition, without which one is not of the world, or false gallantry,

without which one is lacking in spirit. For it is the greatest misery in human affairs that no one contents himself
with being absurd himself, but we must pass along our folly
to others, so much so that things indifferent to us often
attract our imprudent curiosity by their fame. Sometimes
a clever libel, sometimes an agreeable portrait of an evil
action imposes itself upon our mind. Thus, in that strange
hurry to communicate our follies to one another, the most
innocent souls take on the color of vice and gather up
evil here and there in the world, collecting the errors that
cloud our intellect little by little, just as unhealthy germs
are taken in from a table laden with spoiled meats. Such is,
more or less, the seduction that reigns openly in the world,
and if you ask Tertullian what he fears for us from such a
school, "everything," he responds, "including the air, which
is infected by so much evil speech, and by so many corrupt
maxims."

Save us, save us Lord, from contagion by our age: "Help,
Lord; for there is no longer any that is godly; for the faithful have vanished from among the sons of men" (Ps 12:1).
Now we must not persuade ourselves that he is lamenting
infidels and idolaters. These not only diminish the truth,
they have disdain for it. He is lamenting the children of
God, who, not being able completely to extinguish truth
because of the evidence they possess, trim and hem it
according to the pleasure of their passions. For does not the
world attempt to pick and choose its vices? There are some
which we willingly loathe and leave to public hatred such
as avarice, cruelty, and treason. There are others which we

attempt to honor, such as those delicate passions we call the vices of a gentleman. Miserable men: what are you trying to do? "Is Christ divided?" (1 Cor 1:13) What did he do to you, this Jesus, that you would boldly rip up and mutilate his teaching by these harmful distinctions? Is not the same God who is the protector of truthfulness also the author of temperance? "Jesus Christ is the whole of wisdom," says Tertullian, "of light, and of truth; why do you divide him by your lying" as if his holy Gospel were but a monstrous assemblage of the true and the false, as if his Justice had allowed some crime to escape censure.

Whence comes so great a disorder unless the truth has been diminished. She is diminished in her purity because she is mixed with falsehoods, diminished in her integrity because she is maimed and cut into, diminished in her majesty because, instead of carefully studying her, we lose the respect that is due to her. We have taken away so much of her grandeur that we scarcely notice her. Her great stars seem to us like little points of light, so far do we put her away from us and so much is our vision of her obscured by the clouds of our ignorance and by our own cherished opinions!

Because the teachings of the Gospel are so greatly diminished in our age, and because the whole world conspires against them and cripples them by so many evil habits of mind, God, in his supreme justice, has had to provide for their defense and to raise up advocates to plead her cause. It is for this reason that pulpits are built near the altars, so that while the truth is so boldly attacked in the company of the worldly, there should be at least one place where men speak openly in her favor and that the most just cause not be the one that is the most neglected. Come then to listen attentively to the defense of the truth from the mouths of preachers. Come to receive from their ministry the word of Jesus Christ condemning the world and its vices, its customs, and its anti-Christian teachings. God has ordained two things for us, to listen to and to act upon his holy word. But will we have the courage to practice what we cannot bear to hear? Will we open our hearts, if we close our ears? Can we choose something to which we refuse to pay attention?

It is this attention itself that we must now consider.

II

When the truth shall come to be our judge, it will not appear to our senses or need any articulate sound for us to understand it. It will be in our consciences, even in the consciences of the greatest of sinners, where, in this life, it is often ignored. What shall happen after death? Truth will make itself known, and its sentence shall be pronounced. Imagine what will be their surprise, how strange and terrible it will be, when the holy truths which sinners considered useless and scarcely even thought about, will blaze in their eyes all at once, showing them both their sins and the law, so that they will see the enormity of their sins by their contrast with the truth and will tremble with shame for their actions while recognizing that their punishment is deserved.

"Knowing the fear of the Lord, we persuade men" (2 Cor 5:11). We come to exhort them, on God's behalf, to listen to the truths of the Gospel and willingly to apply their minds to them.

You who say that you already know everything and that you do not need to be preached to, merely show that you are unaware of the cast of your own minds. The human mind is an infinite abyss, yet it is too small and narrow to comprehend itself, for its thoughts are so sinuous, its recesses so deep, its memories so hidden, that often its own lights are less present to itself than are foreign ones. We so often fail to think about what we know and keep at arm's length what is already deep within us, and thus we come to lack what we had possessed. The soul, as St. Augustine said, is too small to possess itself. Let us prove it by means of an example.

What was the deep cavern into which David's perfect knowledge of the laws of humanity and justice had fallen when Nathan the prophet had to be sent to remind him of them? Nathan spoke to him. Nathan conversed with him, but David was so captivated by his passion and so distracted by his work that he had forgotten the truth, and thus he understood little of what he heard. The prophet, therefore, was at last forced to say to him "You are the man" (2 Sam 12:7). Was David then aware of what he knew? Was he understanding what he heard? Do not believe my account, but rather his own testimony. He himself was astonished to realize that his own lights had abandoned him during this miserable time: "the light of my eyes—it also has gone from me" (Ps 38:10). He was not speaking about someone else's light, but the light of his own eyes, that was the one he had lost. Listen, wise man, you who do not need to be preached to: your own knowledge has left you, you do not have the light. Perhaps you have the light of knowledge, but you do not have the light of recollection, and your knowledge is not lighting up the darkness or chasing away the shadows.

Do not tell me that you already have perfect understanding of the truths that you need to know, for I have no wish to contradict you. Well then, you have eyes, but they are shut. The truth of God is in your mind like a great torch, but it is not burning. You must allow us to come to open your eyes, heavy with sleep, so that you may see what you need to see. Allow the preachers of the Gospel to tell you about the truth of salvation, so that the blessed encounter of your thoughts with theirs will prompt you to be thoughtful, so that their spark may relight your smoldering torch.

How often it happens that we complain about things we used to know not coming readily to mind or that forgetfulness, shock, or emotion should hinder our knowledge from having its proper effect. From these experiences, we know that the truths by which we ought to live need to be frequently stirred up by admonitions. If they are not, if these truths are allowed to slumber, they lose the habit of coming to mind and become powerless, sterile, and useless ornaments of our memory.

It is, indeed, not a small part of our malady that the

holy truths of the Christian faith are so quickly lost in the depths of our minds. For although they do not require much from our memory—being detached from our senses—our neglect of them prevents us from taking them to heart and being penetrated by them as we ought. To the contrary, we almost pride ourselves in setting them aside with a sort of affected disdain, as the Psalmist says: "they have set their eyes bowing down to the earth" (Ps 17:11, Douay-Rheims). Note that he says "they have set," that is, when the truth of salvation presents itself to us in order to raise our sights to heaven, we turn our eyes to the earth by a deliberate choice and a determined will. It is, therefore, necessary that those who preach the Gospel should by their admonitions restore to our eyes what they had lost.

You yourselves should help them in this work that is so useful to your salvation by practicing what it says in Ecclesiasticus: "A man of sense will praise every wise word he shall hear, and will apply it to himself" (Sirach 21:17, Douay-Rheims). The prudent man is not content to praise wisdom, nor to look about to see whether there is someone else to whom he may apply it. He does not trifle with the one speaking by giving his own interpretation of what is said. No, he believes that he is the one spoken to, and, in truth, whomever senses within himself that his own vice is being attacked should believe that the entire discourse is addressed to himself alone. If from time to time we sense something that cuts us, and that across our wandering ways and conflicted passions touches us on our secret wound and finds in the depth of our heart a sin that we are covering up, it is then that we must listen attentively to Christ, who comes to take away from us our false sense of peace and who places his hand upon our very wound. This is the time when we must follow the counsel of the wise man and apply the words to ourselves. If the blow does not strike deep enough, we must take up the sword and drive it home. May it please God to enter so deeply into our wound that our heart will be wrung with compunction, that blood from the wound will pour from our eyes in the form of the tears that St. Augustine so rightly called the blood of the soul. For it is then that Jesus will have preached to us, and we will have experienced the final effect of preaching, which will be the subject of just a few more words of mine.

III

When I consider why sacred discourses, which are so full of needful advice, are nevertheless so ineffectual, the following reason seems the most likely to me. It is that men and women today are so confident in their own good sense that they do not think they are able to be persuaded to adopt a conclusion they do not already hold. Moreover, not being moved by the truth that shines in their consciences, they are not open to being moved by words spoken by another. And so, if they listen to preaching at all, it is either as to an indifferent sort of speech that they hear as a matter of conformity to custom, or, at best, as an agreeable amusement, which does nothing more than tickle their ears with a certain passing pleasure.

To disabuse ourselves of such a cast of mind, let us consider that the word of the Gospel—given to us directly by God—is no mere sound to be dispersed in the air, but an instrument of grace. Place as high a value as you wish upon the spoken word as we find it in human affairs. Let it be the interpreter of every thought, the mediator of every agreement, the pledge of good faith, and the bond of all commerce. It is both more necessary and more effective in the ministry of our religion, and here is the proof of that claim. It is a fundamental truth that we cannot obtain grace other than by the means that have been established by God. And it was the Son of God himself, the unique mediator of our salvation, who chose the word to be the instrument of his grace and the universal tool of his Holy Spirit for the sanctification of souls. Open your eyes and contemplate all that the Church has that is most sacred, the baptismal fonts, the tribunes of penance, the most holy altars: it is the word of Jesus Christ that regenerates the children of God, that absolves them from their sins, and that prepares for them an immortal food upon these holy altars. If that word acts so powerfully in the fonts, confessionals, and altars, then surely it cannot be useless in the pulpit. There it acts in another manner, but it remains the tool of the Spirit of God. Who is unaware of this fact? It is by the preaching of the Gospel that the all-powerful Spirit gave disciples, followers, and children to Christ. If it was necessary to cast fear into the hearts of criminals, the word thundered. If it was necessary to captivate the understanding, the word was a chain by which the hearers were drawn to Christ crucified. If it was necessary to pierce hearts with divine love, the word was an arrow to make the saving wound: "your arrows are sharp" (Ps 45:5). The word has established the Faith, ordered the people in obedience, toppled idols, and converted the world.

Yet all these achievements were in the past, and today all that remains of them is their memory. Christ is no longer attended, or, if he is, it is so negligently that more attention is given to useless speech than to his. His word is everywhere seeking souls who will receive it, and everywhere finds an invincible hardness of hearts that are too preoccupied to give him entrance.

It is not that we fail to attend Mass. Our churches will be full during these holy forty days, and some people will even lend an attentive ear to the sacred discourses they will hear. Yet how many will there be, as the Son of God said, who in seeing will not see and in hearing will not hear! (Mt 13:13) St. Augustine explained that preaching is a great mystery: "the sound of the word strikes from without, but the Master is within." True preaching is accomplished in the heart. And so, to hear the preaching of Christ, we need not stir up our attention to the cadence of the preacher, but to what in his preaching will bring order to our lives. We must not rest in the pleasure of beautiful thoughts, but we must ensure that our desires are rectified. Nor does it suffice that we judge aright, we must make resolutions. And, if there is a place hidden deep within where all of our designs are set, and from which all of our movement proceeds, it is there that the divine word must do salutary damage to us by smashing all of our idols, toppling every altar on which creatures are adored, spilling all of the incense that we burn to them, and chasing off all of the sacrifices that we make to them, so that upon all of this debris the victorious throne of Christ may be raised. If not, we have not heard the preaching of Jesus.

It is for this reason, alas, that Christ has so few listeners, and that within the crowd of the many who press upon him, he has so few disciples. For in truth, either we listen coldly, or the words prompt only a feeble response that is a mere likeness of true conviction, and sterile desires that remain always desires and do not become resolutions, guttering flames that do not catch and burn the tinder, but dance above it until they are extinguished by the merest breeze. We are like "the Ephraimites, armed with the bow," who "turned back on the day of battle" (Ps 78:9). While listening to the word, they formed great plans and seemed to be sharpening their arms to oppose their vices, but in the day of temptation they acted shamefully. They promised much during maneuvers, but quickly folded during combat. They seemed alert when the trumpet sounded, but turned their backs as soon as fighting began.

Shall I say what I think of this? Such weak and imperfect emotions that are gone after a moment are worthy to be formed in front of the stage, where mere illusions are played out, and not before the Gospel pulpit, where the holy truth of God appears in its purity. For what has the right of touching our hearts if not the truth? It is the truth that will appear to every rebellious heart on the last day, and then we will all know just how deeply the truth moves us. "When they see him," that is, Christ, "they will be shaken with dreadful fear" (Wis 5:2). They will be troubled and anguished; they will want to hide in the abyss. Why will they be troubled? Because the truth will press upon them. Why will they want to flee? Because the truth will pursue them. Will we find you wherever we go, O persecuting truth? Yes, even in the depths of the abyss, for there the truth will be a horrid spectacle in their eyes, an unbearable weight upon their consciences, and an ever-burning flame in their bowels. Who will give us the grace to be touched by the truth today, so that we will not then be touched in that furious and desperate way? O God, make your word to be effective. O God, you can see the place where I am preaching and know what I ought to say. Give me words of wisdom, give me words of power, give me prudence, courage, skill, and rectitude. You know, O living God, that the ardent zeal that moves me to serve my king causes me to cleave to the task of announcing your Gospel to this great monarch, truly great, and worthy, by the greatness of his soul, of hearing only great things, and worthy, by the love he has for the truth, of never being deceived.

Sire, it is God who should speak from his pulpit. Let him do so by his Holy Spirit, for he alone can do so great a work as to make the man disappear so that God himself can speak his Gospel in all its purity, and make divine all who listen to him, especially Your Majesty, who, already having the honor of representing him on earth, should aspire to the honor of being like him in eternity, by seeing him face to

face, as he is, and according to the immensity of his glory,
which is what I pray for you, in the name of the Father, and
of the Son, and of the Holy Spirit.

Blessed John Henry Cardinal Newman

THE SECOND SPRING

The world grows old, but the Church is ever young.

In 1850, Pius IX restored the Roman Catholic hierarchy in England. That country suddenly enjoyed the official apostolic presence that had been absent for over 250 years. Such an event was certainly good news. Yet it also constituted something of a crisis, insofar as it presented a moment of decision and time for choosing.

Father John Henry Newman, the country's most famous convert to Catholicism, was asked to preach to the clergy at the 1852 Provincial Synod of the newly established diocese of Westminster. While giving thanks for the "Second Spring," Newman understood that for the official restoration of the hierarchy to take root and bear fruit, it needed to be sown in the soil of faith and zeal. Thus, his sermon seeks both to inspire and to strengthen the gathered clergy for the work and challenges before them.

❄   ❄   ❄

THE SECOND SPRING

"ARISE, MAKE HASTE, my love, my dove, my beautiful one, and come. For the winter is now past, the rain is over and gone. The flowers have appeared in our land." (Cant., ii. 10-12).

We have familiar experience of the order, the constancy, the perpetual renovation of the material world which surrounds us. Frail and transitory as is every part of it, restless and migratory as are its elements, never-ceasing as are its changes, still it abides. It is bound together by a law of permanence, it is set up in unity; and, though it is ever dying, it is ever coming to life again. Dissolution does but give birth to fresh modes of organization, and one death is the parent of a thousand lives. Each hour, as it comes, is but a testimony, how fleeting, yet how secure, how certain, is the great whole. It is like an image on the waters, which is ever the same, though the waters ever flow. Change upon change—yet one change cries out to another, like the alternate Seraphim, in praise and in glory of their Maker. The sun sinks to rise again; the day is swallowed up in the gloom of the night, to be born out of it, as fresh as if it had never been quenched. Spring passes into summer, and through summer and autumn into winter, only the more surely, by its own ultimate return, to triumph over that grave, towards which it resolutely hastened from its first hour. We mourn over the blossoms of May, because they are to wither; but we know, withal, that May is one day to have its revenge upon November, by the revolution of that solemn circle which never stops—which teaches us in our height of hope, ever to be sober, and in our depth of desolation, never to despair.

And forcibly as this comes home to every one of us, not less forcible is the contrast which exists between this material world, so vigorous, so reproductive, amid all its changes, and the moral world, so feeble, so downward, so resourceless, amid all its aspirations. That which ought to come to nought, endures; that which promises a future, disappoints and is no more. The same sun shines in heaven from first to last, and the blue firmament, the everlasting mountains, reflect his rays; but where is there upon earth the champion, the hero, the lawgiver, the body politic, the sovereign race, which was great three hundred years ago, and is great now? Moralists and poets, often do they descant upon this innate vitality of matter, this innate perishableness of mind. Man rises to fall: he tends to dissolution from the moment he begins to be; he lives on, indeed, in his children, he lives on in his name, he lives not on in his own person. He is, as regards the manifestations of his nature here below, as a bubble that breaks, and as water poured out upon the earth. He was young, he is old, he is never young again. This is the lament over him, poured forth in verse and in prose, by Christians and by heathen. The greatest work of God's hands under the sun, he, in all the manifestations of his complex being, is born only to die.

His bodily frame first begins to feel the power of this constraining law, though it is the last to succumb to it. We look at the bloom of youth with interest, yet with pity; and the more graceful and sweet it is, with pity so much the more; for, whatever be its excellence and its glory, soon it begins to be deformed and dishonoured by the very force of its living on. It grows into exhaustion and collapse, till at length it crumbles into that dust out of which it was originally taken.

So is it, too, with our moral being, a far higher and diviner portion of our natural constitution; it begins with life, it ends with what is worse than the mere loss of life, with a living death. How beautiful is the human heart, when it puts forth its first leaves, and opens and rejoices in its spring-tide. Fair as may be the bodily form, fairer far, in its green foliage and bright blossoms, is natural virtue. It blooms in the young, like some rich flower, so delicate, so fragrant, and so dazzling. Generosity and lightness of heart and amiableness, the confiding spirit, the gentle temper, the elastic cheerfulness, the open hand, the pure affection, the noble aspiration, the heroic resolve, the romantic pursuit, the love in which self has no part,—are not these beautiful? and are they not dressed up and set forth for admiration in their best shapes, in tales and in poems? and ah! what a prospect of good is there! who could believe that it is to fade! and yet, as night follows upon day, as decrepitude follows upon health, so surely are failure, and overthrow, and annihilation, the issue of this natural virtue, if time only be allowed to it to run its course. There are those who are cut off in the first opening of this excellence, and then, if we may trust their epitaphs, they have lived like angels; but wait a while, let them live on, let the course of life proceed, let the bright soul go through the fire and water of the world's temptations and seductions and corruptions and transformations; and, alas for the insufficiency of nature! alas for its powerlessness to persevere, its waywardness in disappointing its own promise! Wait till youth has become age; and not more different is the miniature which we have of him when a boy, when every feature spoke of hope, put side by side of the large portrait painted to his honour, when he is old, when his limbs are shrunk, his eye dim, his brow furrowed, and his hair grey, than differs the moral grace of that boyhood from the forbidding and repulsive aspect of his soul, now that he has lived to the age of man. For moroseness, and misanthropy, and selfishness, is the ordinary winter of that spring.

Such is man in his own nature, and such, too, is he in his works. The noblest efforts of his genius, the conquests he has made, the doctrines he has originated, the nations he has civilized, the states he has created, they outlive himself, they outlive him by many centuries, but they tend to an end, and that end is dissolution. Powers of the world, sovereignties, dynasties, sooner or later come to nought; they have their fatal hour. The Roman conqueror shed tears over Carthage, for in the destruction of the rival city he discerned too truly an augury of the fall of Rome; and at length, with the weight and the responsibilities, the crimes and the glories, of centuries upon centuries, the Imperial City fell.

Thus man and all his works are mortal; they die, and they have no power of renovation.

But what is it, my Fathers, my Brothers, what is it that has happened in England just at this time? Something strange is passing over this land, by the very surprise, by the very commotion, which it excites. Were we not near enough the scene of action to be able to say what is going on,— were we the inhabitants of some sister planet possessed of a more perfect mechanism than this earth has discovered for surveying the transactions of another globe,—and did we turn our eyes thence towards England just at this season, we should be arrested by a political phenomenon as wonderful as any which the astronomer notes down from his physical field of view. It would be the occurrence of a national commotion, almost without parallel, more violent than has happened here for centuries,—at least in the judgments and intentions of men, if not in act and deed. We should note it down, that soon after St. Michael's day, 1850, a storm arose in the moral world, so furious as to demand some great explanation, and to rouse in us an intense desire to gain it. We should observe it increasing from day to day, and spreading from place to place, without remission, almost without lull, up to this very hour, when perhaps it threatens worse still, or at least gives no sure prospect of alleviation. Every party in the body politic undergoes its influence,— from the Queen upon her throne, down to the little ones in the infant or day school. The ten thousands of the constituency, the sum-total of Protestant sects, the aggregate of religious societies and associations, the great body of established clergy in town and country, the bar, even the medical profession, nay, even literary and scientific circles, every

class, every interest, every fireside, gives tokens of this ubiq-
uitous storm. This would be our report of it, seeing it from
the distance, and we should speculate on the cause. What
is it all about? against what is it directed? what wonder has
happened upon earth? what prodigious, what preternatural
event is adequate to the burden of so vast an effect?

We should judge rightly in our curiosity about a phenomenon like this; it must be a portentous event, and it is.
It is an innovation, a miracle, I may say, in the course of
human events. The physical world revolves year by year, and
begins again; but the political order of things does not renew
itself, does not return; it continues, but it proceeds; there is
no retrogression. This is so well understood by men of the
day, that with them progress is idolized as another name for
good. The past never returns—it is never good;—if we are
to escape existing ills, it must be by going forward. The past
is out of date; the past is dead. As well may the dead live
to us, well may the dead profit us, as the past return. This,
then, is the cause of this national transport, this national
cry, which encompasses us. The past has returned, the dead
lives. Thrones are overturned, and are never restored; States
live and die, and then are matter only for history. Babylon
was great, and Tyre, and Egypt, and Nineve, and shall never
be great again. The English Church was, and the English
Church was not, and the English Church is once again.
This is the portent, worthy of a cry. It is the coming in of a
Second Spring; it is a restoration in the moral world, such
as that which yearly takes place in the physical.

Three centuries ago, and the Catholic Church, that

great creation of God's power, stood in this land in pride of place. It had the honours of near a thousand years upon it; it was enthroned on some twenty sees up and down the broad country; it was based in the will of a faithful people; it energized through ten thousand instruments of power and influence; and it was ennobled by a host of Saints and Martyrs. The churches, one by one, recounted and rejoiced in the line of glorified intercessors, who were the respective objects of their grateful homage. Canterbury alone numbered perhaps some sixteen, from St. Augustine to St. Dunstan and St. Elphege, from St. Anselm and St. Thomas down to St. Edmund. York had its St. Paulinus, St. John, St. Wilfrid, and St. William; London, its St. Erconwald; Durham, its St. Cuthbert; Winton, its St. Swithun. Then there were St. Aidan of Lindisfarne, and St. Hugh of Lincoln, and St. Chad of Lichfield, and St. Thomas of Hereford, and St. Oswald and St. Wulstan of Worcester, and St. Osmund of Salisbury, and St. Birinus of Dorchester, and St. Richard of Chichester. And then, too, its religious orders, its monastic establishments, its universities, its wide relations all over Europe, its high prerogatives in the temporal state, its wealth, its dependencies, its popular honours,—where was there in the whole of Christendom a more glorious hierarchy? Mixed up with the civil institutions, with kings and nobles, with the people, found in every village and in every town,—it seemed destined to stand, so long as England stood, and to outlast, it might be, England's greatness.

But it was the high decree of heaven, that the majesty of that presence should be blotted out. It is a long story, my Fathers and Brothers—you know it well. I need not go through it. The vivifying principle of truth, the shadow of St. Peter, the grace of the Redeemer, left it. That old Church in its day became a corpse (a marvellous, an awful change!); and then it did but corrupt the air which once it refreshed, and cumber the ground which once it beautified. So all seemed to be lost; and there was a struggle for a time, and then its priests were cast out or martyred. There were sacrileges innumerable. Its temples were profaned or destroyed; its revenues seized by covetous nobles, or squandered upon the ministers of a new faith. The presence of Catholicism was at length simply removed,—its grace disowned,—its power despised,—its name, except as a matter of history, at length almost unknown. It took a long time to do this thoroughly; much time, much thought, much labour, much expense; but at last it was done. Oh, that miserable day, centuries before we were born! What a martyrdom to live in it and see the fair form of Truth, moral and material, hacked piecemeal, and every limb and organ carried off, and burned in the fire, or cast into the deep! But at last the work was done. Truth was disposed of, and shovelled away, and there was a calm, a silence, a sort of peace;—and such was about the state of things when we were born into this weary world.

My Fathers and Brothers, you have seen it on one side, and some of us on another; but one and all of us can bear witness to the fact of the utter contempt into which Catholicism had fallen by the time that we were born. You, alas, know it far better than I can know it; but it may not be out of place, if by one or two tokens, as by the strokes of a pencil, I bear witness to you from without, of what you can witness so much more truly from within. No longer the Catholic Church in the country; nay, no longer, I may say, a Catholic community;—but a few adherents of the Old Religion, moving silently and sorrowfully about, as memorials of what had been. "The Roman Catholics;"—not a sect, not even an interest, as men conceived of it,—not a body, however small, representative of the Great Communion abroad,—but a mere handful of individuals, who might be counted, like the pebbles and detritus of the great deluge, and who, forsooth, merely happened to retain a creed which, in its day indeed, was the profession of a Church. Here a set of poor Irishmen, coming and going at harvest time, or a colony of them lodged in a miserable quarter of the vast metropolis. There, perhaps an elderly person, seen walking in the streets, grave and solitary, and strange, though noble in bearing, and said to be of good family, and a "Roman Catholic." An old-fashioned house of gloomy appearance, closed in with high walls, with an iron gate, and yews, and the report attaching to it that "Roman Catholics" lived there; but who they were, or what they did, or what was meant by calling them Roman Catholics, no one could tell;—though it had an unpleasant sound, and told of form and superstition. And then, perhaps, as we went to and fro, looking with a boy's curious eyes through the great city, we might come today upon some Moravian chapel, or Quaker's meeting-house, and tomorrow on a chapel of the "Roman Catholics": but nothing was to be gathered from it, except that there were lights burning there, and some boys in white, swinging censers; and what it all meant could only be learned from books, from Protestant Histories and Sermons; and they did not report well of "the Roman Catholics," but, on the contrary, deposed that they had once had power and had abused it. And then, again, we might on one occasion hear it pointedly put out by some literary man, as the result of his careful investigation, and as a recondite point of information, which few knew, that there was this difference between the Roman Catholics of England and the Roman Catholics of Ireland, that the latter had bishops, and the former were governed by four officials, called Vicars-Apostolic.

Such was about the sort of knowledge possessed of Christianity by the heathen of old time, who persecuted its adherents from the face of the earth, and then called them a *gens lucifuga*, a people who shunned the light of day. Such were Catholics in England, found in corners, and alleys, and cellars, and the housetops, or in the recesses of the country; cut off from the populous world around them, and dimly seen, as if through a mist or in twilight, as ghosts flitting to and fro, by the high Protestants, the lords of the earth. At length so feeble did they become, so utterly contemptible, that contempt gave birth to pity; and the more generous of their tyrants actually began to wish to bestow on them some favour, under the notion that their opinions were simply too absurd ever to spread again, and that they themselves, were they but raised in civil importance, would soon unlearn and be ashamed of them. And thus, out of mere kindness to us, they began to vilify our doctrines to the Protestant world, that so our very idiocy or our secret unbelief might be our plea for mercy.

A great change, an awful contrast, between the time-honoured Church of St. Augustine and St. Thomas, and the poor remnant of their children in the beginning of the nine-teenth century! It was a miracle, I might say, to have pulled down that lordly power; but there was a greater and a truer one in store. No one could have prophesied its fall, but still less would any one have ventured to prophesy its rise again. The fall was wonderful; still after all it was in the order of nature;—all things come to nought: its rise again would be a different sort of wonder, for it is in the order of grace,—and who can hope for miracles, and such a miracle as this? Has the whole course of history a like to show? I must speak cautiously and according to my knowledge, but I recollect no parallel to it. Augustine, indeed, came to the same island to which the early missionaries had come already; but they came to Britons, and he to Saxons. The Arian Goths and Lombards, too, cast off their heresy in St. Augustine's age, and joined the Church; but they had never fallen away from her. The inspired word seems to imply the almost impossi-bility of such a grace as the renovation of those who have crucified to themselves again, and trodden under foot, the Son of God. Who then could have dared to hope that, out of so sacrilegious a nation as this is, a people would have been formed again unto their Saviour? What signs did it show that it was to be singled out from among the nations? Had it been prophesied some fifty years ago, would not the very notion have seemed preposterous and wild?

My Fathers, there was one of your own order, then in the maturity of his powers and his reputation. His name is the property of this diocese; yet is too great, too venerable, too dear to all Catholics, to be confined to any part of England, when it is rather a household word in the mouths of all of us. What would have been the feelings of that venerable man, the champion of God's ark in an evil time, could he have lived to see this day? It is almost presumptuous for one who knew him not, to draw pictures about him, and his thoughts, and his friends, some of whom are even here present; yet am I wrong in fancying that a day such as this, in which we stand, would have seemed to him a dream, or, if he prophesied of it, to his hearers nothing but a mockery? Say that one time, rapt in spirit, he had reached forward to the future, and that his mortal eye had wandered from that lowly chapel in the valley which had been for centuries in the possession of Catholics, to the neighbouring height, then waste and solitary. And let him say to those about him: "I see a bleak mount, looking upon an open country, over against that huge town, to whose inhabitants Catholicism is of so little account. I see the ground marked out, and an ample enclosure made; and plantations are rising there, clothing and circling in the space.

"And there on that high spot, far from the haunts of men, yet in the very centre of the island, a large edifice, or rather pile of edifices, appears with many fronts, and courts, and long cloisters and corridors, and story upon story. And there it rises, under the invocation of the same sweet and powerful name which has been our strength and consolation in the Valley. I look more attentively at that building, and I see it is fashioned upon that ancient style of art which brings back the past, which had seemed to be perishing from off the face of the earth, or to be preserved only as a curiosity, or to be imitated only as a fancy. I listen, and I hear the sound of voices, grave and musical, renewing the old chant, with which Augustine greeted Ethelbert in the free air upon the Kentish strand. It comes from a long procession, and it winds along the cloisters. Priests and Religious, theologians from the schools, and canons from the Cathedral, walk in due precedence. And then there comes a vision of well-nigh twelve mitred heads; and last I see a Prince of the Church, in the royal dye of empire and of martyrdom, a pledge to us from Rome of Rome's unwearied love, a token that that goodly company is firm in Apostolic faith and hope. And the shadow of the Saints is there;—St. Benedict is there, speaking to us by the voice of bishop and of priest, and counting over the long ages through which he has prayed, and studied, and laboured; there, too, is St. Dominic's white wool, which no blemish can impair, no stain can dim:—and if St. Bernard be not there, it is only that his absence may make him be remembered more. And the princely patriarch, St. Ignatius, too, the St. George of the modern world, with his chivalrous lance run through his writhing foe, he, too, sheds his blessing upon that train. And others, also, his equals or his juniors in history, whose pictures are above our altars, or soon shall be, the surest proof that the Lord's arm has not waxen short, nor His mercy failed,—they, too, are looking down from their thrones on high upon the throng.

And so that high company moves on into the holy place; and there, with august rite and awful sacrifice, inaugurates the great act which brings it thither." What is that act? it is the first synod of a new Hierarchy; it is the resurrection of the Church.

O my Fathers, my Brothers, had that revered Bishop so spoken then, who that had heard him but would have said that he spoke what could not be? What! those few scattered worshippers, the Roman Catholics, to form a Church! Shall the past be rolled back? Shall the grave open? Shall the Saxons live again to God? Shall the shepherds, watching their poor flocks by night, be visited by a multitude of the heavenly army, and hear how their Lord has been new-born in their own city? Yes; for grace can, where nature cannot. The world grows old, but the Church is ever young. She can, in any time, at her Lord's will, "inherit the Gentiles, and inhabit the desolate cities." "Arise, Jerusalem, for thy light is come, and the glory of the Lord is risen upon thee. Behold, darkness shall cover the earth, and a mist the people; but the Lord shall arise upon thee, and His glory shall be seen upon thee. Lift up thine eyes round about, and see; all these are gathered together, they come to thee; thy sons shall come from afar, and thy daughters shall rise up at thy side." "Arise, make haste, my love, my dove, my beautiful one, and come. For the winter is now past, and the rain is over and gone. The flowers have appeared in our land . . . the fig-tree hath put forth her green figs; the vines in flower yield their sweet smell. Arise, my love, my beautiful one, and come." It is the time for thy Visitation. Arise, Mary, and go forth in thy strength into that north country, which once was thine own, and take possession of a land which knows thee not. Arise, Mother of God, and with thy thrilling voice, speak to those who labour with child, and are in pain, till the babe of grace leaps within them! Shine on us, dear Lady, with thy bright countenance, like the sun in his strength, O stella matutina, O harbinger of peace, till our year is one perpetual May. From thy sweet eyes, from thy pure smile, from thy majestic brow, let ten thousand influences rain down, not to confound or overwhelm, but to persuade, to win over thine enemies. O Mary, my hope, O Mother undefiled, fulfil to us the promise of this Spring. A second temple rises on the ruins of the old. Canterbury has gone its way, and York is gone, and Durham is gone, and Winchester is gone. It was sore to part with them. We clung to the vision of past greatness, and would not believe it could come to nought; but the Church in England has died, and the Church lives again. Westminster and Nottingham, Beverley and Hexham, Northampton and Shrewsbury, if the world lasts, shall be names as musical to the ear, as stirring to the heart, as the glories we have lost; and Saints shall rise out of them, if God so will, and Doctors once again shall give the law to Israel, and Preachers call to penance and to justice, as at the beginning.

Yes, my Fathers and Brothers, and if it be God's blessed will, not Saints alone, not Doctors only, not Preachers only, shall be ours—but Martyrs, too, shall reconsecrate the soil to God. We know not what is before us, ere we win our own; we are engaged in a great, a joyful work, but in proportion to God's grace is the fury of His enemies. They have welcomed us as the lion greets his prey. Perhaps they may be familiarized in time with our appearance, but perhaps they may be irritated the more. To set up the Church again in England is too great an act to be done in a corner. We have had reason to expect that such a boon would not be given to us without a cross. It is not God's way that great blessings should descend without the sacrifice first of great sufferings. If the truth is to be spread to any wide extent among this people, how can we dream, how can we hope, that trial and trouble shall not accompany its going forth? And we have already, if it may be said without presumption, to commence our work withal, a large store of merits. We have no slight outfit for our opening warfare. Can we religiously suppose that the blood of our martyrs, three centuries ago and since, shall never receive its recompense? Those priests, secular and regular, did they suffer for no end? or rather, for an end which is not yet accomplished? The long imprisonment, the fetid dungeon, the weary suspense, the tyrannous trial, the barbarous sentence, the savage execution, the rack, the gibbet, the knife, the cauldron, the numberless tortures of those holy victims, O my God, are they to have no reward? Are Thy martyrs to cry from under Thine altar for their loving vengeance on this guilty people, and to cry in vain? Shall they lose life, and not gain a better life for the children of those who persecuted them? Is this Thy way, O my God, righteous and true? Is it according to Thy promise, O King of saints, if I may dare talk to Thee of justice? Did not Thou Thyself pray for Thine enemies upon the cross, and convert them? Did not Thy first Martyr win Thy great Apostle, then a persecutor, by his loving prayer? And in that day of trial and desolation for England, when hearts were pierced through and through with Mary's woe, at the crucifixion of Thy body mystical, was not every tear that flowed, and every drop of blood that was shed, the seeds of a future harvest, when they who sowed in sorrow were to reap in joy?

And as that suffering of the Martyrs is not yet recompensed, so, perchance, it is not yet exhausted. Something, for what we know, remains to be undergone, to complete the necessary sacrifice. May God forbid it, for this poor nation's sake! But still could we be surprised, my Fathers and my Brothers, if the winter even now should not yet be quite over? Have we any right to take it strange, if, in this English land, the spring-time of the Church should turn out to be an English spring, an uncertain, anxious time of hope and fear, of joy and suffering,—of bright promise and budding hopes, yet withal, of keen blasts, and cold showers, and sudden storms?

One thing alone I know,—that according to our need, so will be our strength. One thing I am sure of, that the more the enemy rages against us, so much the more will the Saints in Heaven plead for us; the more fearful are our trials from the world, the more present to us will be our Mother Mary, and our good Patrons and Angel Guardians; the more malicious are the devices of men against us, the louder cry of supplication will ascend from the bosom of the whole Church to God for us. We shall not be left orphans; we shall have within us the strength of the Paraclete, promised to the Church and to every member of it. My Fathers, my Brothers in the priesthood, I speak from my heart when I declare my conviction, that there is no one among you here present but, if God so willed, would readily become a martyr for His sake. I do not say you would wish it; I do not say that the natural will would not pray that that chalice might pass away; I do not speak of what you can do by any strength of yours;—but in the strength of God, in the grace of the Spirit, in the armour of justice, by the consolations and peace of the Church, by the blessing of the Apostles Peter and Paul, and in the name of Christ, you would do what nature cannot do. By the intercession of the Saints on high, by the penances and good works and the prayers of the people of God on earth, you would be forcibly borne up as upon the waves of the mighty deep, and carried on out of yourselves by the fulness of grace, whether nature wished it or no. I do not mean violently, or with unseemly struggle, but calmly, gracefully, sweetly, joyously, you would mount up and ride forth to the battle, as on the rush of Angels' wings, as your fathers did before you, and gained the prize. You, who day by day offer up the Immaculate Lamb of God, you who hold in your hands the Incarnate Word under the visible tokens which He has ordained, you who again and again drain the chalice of the Great Victim; who is to make you fear? what is to startle you? what to seduce you? who is to stop you, whether you are to suffer or to do, whether to lay the foundations of the Church in tears, or to put the crown upon the work in jubilation?

My Fathers, my Brothers, one word more. It may seem
as if I were going out of my way in thus addressing you; but
I have some sort of plea to urge in extenuation. When the
English College at Rome was set up by the solicitude of a
great Pontiff in the beginning of England's sorrows, and
missionaries were trained there for confessorship and martyrdom here, who was it that saluted the fair Saxon youths
as they passed by him in the streets of the great city, with
the salutation, "Salvete flores martyrum"? And when the
time came for each in turn to leave that peaceful home,
and to go forth to the conflict, to whom did they betake
themselves before leaving Rome, to receive a blessing which
might nerve them for their work? They went for a Saint's
blessing; they went to a calm old man, who had never seen
blood, except in penance; who had longed indeed to die for
Christ, what time the great St. Francis opened the way to
the far East, but who had been fixed as if a sentinel in the
holy city, and walked up and down for fifty years on one
beat, while his brethren were in the battle. Oh! the fire of
that heart, too great for its frail tenement, which tormented
him to be kept at home when the whole Church was at war!
and therefore came those bright-haired strangers to him,
ere they set out for the scene of their passion, that the full
zeal and love pent up in that burning breast might find a
vent, and flow over, from him who was kept at home, upon
those who were to face the foe. Therefore one by one, each
in his turn, those youthful soldiers came to the old man;
and one by one they persevered and gained the crown and

the palm,—all but one, who had not gone, and would not go, for the salutary blessing.

My Fathers, my Brothers, that old man was my own St. Philip. Bear with me for his sake. If I have spoken too seriously, his sweet smile shall temper it. As he was with you three centuries ago in Rome, when our Temple fell, so now surely when it is rising, it is a pleasant token that he should have even set out on his travels to you; and that, as if remembering how he interceded for you at home, and recognizing the relations he then formed with you, he should now be wishing to have a name among you, and to be loved by you, and perchance to do you a service, here in your own land.

Blessed Clemens Cardinal von Galen

AGAINST EUTHANASIA

*Time for us to make the divine command-
ments the guiding principles of our lives.*

BORN OF GERMAN nobility, Clemens von Galen gave himself to the service of the Church and to the many threat-
ened by the Third Reich. As bishop of Münster, he spoke
out courageously and constantly against Nazi atrocities. His
fierce opposition earned him the title *Lion of Münster*.

Von Galen's greatest hour came in the summer of 1941,
as the Nazis became more brazen in their crimes. The bishop
first resisted and condemned their seizure of religious houses
in his diocese. Then, despite the persecution his resistance
invited, he preached strongly against the Nazis' euthanizing
of the mentally ill. His sermons are notable not so much
for their eloquence or style but for their strength and courage. His words served as both a rebuke to the Nazis and an

inspiration to all suffering under their regime. On August 3, 1941, he preached the following, perhaps his strongest and most famous sermon.

❧   ❧   ❧

AGAINST EUTHANASIA

After the reading of the Gospel of the day, the ninth Sunday after Pentecost, "When Jesus had come near to Jerusalem and seen the city, He wept over it . . ." (Lk 19: 41–47).

M Y DEAR DIOCESANS! A shocking event is portrayed in today's Gospel. Jesus weeps! The Son of God weeps! A person weeps who is in pain, pain of body or pain of heart. At that time, Jesus was not yet suffering in body, and yet He wept. How great must have been the pain of soul, the sorrow of heart, of this bravest of men, that He wept!

Why did He weep? He wept over Jerusalem, over the holy city, so dear to Himself, the capital city of His people. He wept over its inhabitants, His fellow countrymen, because they did not want to recognize that which alone could prevent the punishment that He could see with His omniscience and that His divine justice had predetermined: "If only you knew the things that would serve for your peace!" Why do the inhabitants of Jerusalem not recognize this? Not long before, Jesus had said, "Jerusalem, Jerusalem! How often would I have gathered your children together, as a hen gathers her chicks under her wings, but you would not!" (Lk 13:34) You would not. I, your king, your God, I would. But you would not. How sheltered, how guarded, how protected is the chick beneath the wings of the hen! She keeps it warm, she nourishes it, she defends it. Thus would I protect you, shelter you, defend you against every kind of trouble. I would. You would not! That is why Jesus weeps, that is why this strong man weeps, that is why God weeps. Over the foolishness, the unrighteousness, the crime of this *not-willing*. And over the calamity that would come from it, which His omniscience saw coming, which His justice must decree, if man sets his *not-willing* against all the commandments of God, all the warnings of his conscience, all the loving invitations of the divine Friend, the best of Fathers: "If only you recognized, today, on this day, what would serve for your peace! But you would not." It is something frightening, something unbelievably unjust and leading to destruction, when man places his will against God's will! I would; you would not. That is why Jesus weeps over Jerusalem.

Devout Christians! In the joint pastoral letter of the German Bishops of June 26, 1941, read out on July 6th of this year in all Catholic Churches in Germany, it says among other things:

> To be sure, in Catholic moral teaching there are positive commandments that do not bind when their fulfilment would be connected with great difficulties. But there are also holy obligations of conscience from

which no one can exempt us, which we must fulfill at
whatever cost, even at the cost of our own lives: never,
under any circumstances, outside of war and justified
self-defence, can someone kill an innocent person.

Already on July 6th I had the occasion to add the following
explanation to this joint pastoral letter:

> For several months we have heard reports that patients
> of hospitals and institutes for the mentally ill, patients
> who have been sick for a long time and perhaps seem
> to be incurable, have been compulsorily transferred
> to other locations on orders from Berlin. Regularly
> it happens that after a short time the relatives receive
> notice that the patient has died, the body has been
> cremated, and the ashes can be picked up. The opin-
> ion, bordering on certainty, is held everywhere, that
> these numerous unexpected deaths of the mentally ill
> are not the result of natural causes, but are deliber-
> ately brought about; that in these cases that doctrine
> is being followed, that one can put an end to so-called
> "worthless life," that is, can kill innocent persons if
> one believes that their life is of no more value to the
> people and the state; a horrible doctrine, that would
> justify the murder of the innocent, that gives a funda-
> mental license for the violent killing of those invalids,
> cripples, incurable sick, and weak old persons who are
> no longer able to work!

As I have recently learned from reliable sources, there are

now lists of such patients in hospitals and care centres in the Province of Westphalia, patients who are scheduled to be transported and in a short time put to death as so-called "unproductive fellow-countrymen." The first transport from the institute of Marienthal near Münster took place this week!

German men and women! Section 211 of the Reich Criminal Code still has the force of law. It states, "Anyone who intentionally kills a person, if he has done this with premeditation, is to be punished for murder by death." Perhaps in order to protect those who intentionally kill these poor persons—members of our families—from the punishment prescribed by this law, the sick who are chosen to be killed are transported from the *Heimat* to a distant institution. Then some disease or other is given as the cause of death. Since the bodies are immediately cremated, neither the relatives nor the criminal police are able to determine whether there really was such an illness and what was the true cause of death.

I have, however, been assured that there has been absolutely no concern raised either by the Reich Ministry of the Interior or by Dr. Conti in the Office of the Reich Führer of Doctors, about the fact that already a great number of mentally ill patients in Germany are being intentionally killed and will be killed in the future.

The Criminal Code states in Section 139: "Anyone who has credible knowledge of a plan ... for a crime against life ... and fails to warn the authorities or the endangered person in good time ... is to be punished."

When I heard of the plans to transport sick persons from Marienthal in order to kill them, I bore witness on July 28th to the public prosecutor and police chief of Münster by letters that read as follows:

> According to credible evidence given to me, it is planned during the course of this week (the 31st of July is spoken of) to transfer a great number of patients from the Provincial Health Centre of Marienthal near Münster to the Health Centre of Eichberg, as so-called "unproductive fellow-countrymen," in order soon afterwards to have them deliberately put to death, as has happened, according to universal opinion, in the case of such transfers of patients from other institutes. As such an action violates not only the divine and natural moral law, but also is punishable by death as murder according to section 211 of the Reich Criminal Code, I now give witness as required of me by section 139 of the Reich Criminal Code, and ask that the threatened fellow-countrymen be given immediate protection against those who are planning the transferral and murder, and that I be informed of the actions taken.

I have received no information about the steps taken by the prosecutor or the police.

Already on the 26th of July I had made a most earnest appeal to the Provincial Administration of the Province of Westphalia, which is responsible for these institutions, to which the sick are sent for *care* and *healing*. It was no use! The first transport of innocent victims condemned to death has gone from Marienthal! And I have heard that 800 patients have been transported from the Institute for Care and Healing of Warstein.

So we must assume that these poor, defenseless sick people will sooner or later be killed. Why? Not because they have committed a capital crime; not because they have attacked their caregivers in such wise that these were left with no recourse to save their own lives in self-defence other than the use of violence against their attackers. These would be cases in which, in addition to the killing of armed enemies in a just war, use of force even to the extent of killing is allowed and, not rarely, required. No, not for such reasons do these unfortunate sick people have to die, but rather because, according to the judgment of some official, according to the opinion of some commission, they have become "unworthy of life"; because according to this opinion they belong to the category of "unproductive" fellow countrymen. It is judged that they can no longer produce goods; they are like an old machine that does not work anymore; they are like an old horse that has become incurably lame; they are like a cow that no longer gives milk. What does one do with such old machines? They are scrapped. What does one do with a lame horse or an unproductive cow?

No. I will not continue this comparison to the end, so frightful is its appropriateness and its illuminating power!

We are not dealing with machines, or horses or cows, which are created in order to serve man, to produce goods

for him! One may destroy or kill such beings when they
no longer fulfill this purpose. No, here we are dealing with
people, our fellow human beings, our brothers and sisters!
Poor people, sick people, unproductive people, granted! But
does that mean they have lost the right to life? Do you, do
I, have the right to life only so long as we are productive,
only so long as others acknowledge that we are productive?

If that principle is accepted and made use of, that one
can kill "unproductive" people, then woe to us all, when we
become old and weak! If one can kill unproductive people,
then woe to the disabled who have devoted, risked, and sac-
rificed their healthy bones in the process of production! If
unproductive people can be disposed of by violent means,
then woe to our brave soldiers who return to their homeland severely wounded, as cripples, as invalids! Once it is
granted that people have the right to kill "unproductive"
fellow human beings—even if at the moment it affects
only the poor defenceless mentally ill—then *in principle*
the right has been given to *murder* all unproductive people: the incurably ill, the cripples who are unable to work,
those who have become incapacitated because of work or
war; then the right has been given to murder all of us, once
we become weak with age and therefore unproductive. All
that will be required is for some secret order to come down,
that the process which has been tested on the mentally ill
should now be extended to other "unproductive" people, to
those with incurable lung disease, to the infirm elderly, to
the severely wounded soldiers. Then the life of none of us
is safe. Some commission can put him on the list of the

"unproductive" who are, according to its judgment, "unworthy of life." And no policemen will protect him, and no court will take notice of his murder and subject the murderers to the prescribed punishment! Who will then be able to trust his doctor? Perhaps he will report the patient as "unproductive" and receive the order to kill him. It is unthinkable what degeneration of morals, what universal mistrust will find its way even into the family, if this frightening doctrine is tolerated, taken up, and followed. Woe to humanity, woe to our German people, if the holy commandment of God, "Thou shalt not kill," which the Lord gave on Sinai amid thunder and lightning, which God the Creator wrote into the conscience of man from the beginning, is not only broken, but if this breach is tolerated and taken up as a regular practice without punishment!

I will give you an example of what is now taking place. In Marienthal there was a man of about fifty-five years of age, a farmer from a rural community of the Münsterland—I could give you his name—who has suffered for several years from a mental illness and so was entrusted to the Provincial Health and Care Center of Marienthal for *care*. He was not totally insane; he could receive visits, and was always happy when his relatives came. Fourteen days ago he received a visit from his wife and one of his sons, a soldier on leave from the front. This son is very close to his sick father. So the goodbye was hard. Who knows whether the son will return alive from the war to see his father again?— for he could fall while fighting for his people. No, the son, the soldier, will surely not see his father again on this earth, because the father's name has in the meantime been placed on the list of the unproductive. A relative, who wanted to visit the father this week in Marienthal, was sent away with the news that the sick man, on orders from the Ministry of National Defense, has been moved. No one could answer the question, Where to? The relatives, he was told, will be given news within a few days.

What will the news be? Will it be again, as it has been in other cases? That the man has died, that his body has been cremated, that his ashes can be released in exchange for payment of a fee? Thus, the soldier who is in the field putting his life on the line for his fellow Germans will not see his father again on earth because fellow Germans at home have put his father to death!

What I have just told you are the facts. I can give you the name of the sick man, his wife, his son the soldier, and the place where they live.

"Thou shalt not kill!" God wrote this commandment in the conscience of man long before any book of criminal laws prescribed a punishment for murder, long before any prosecutor accused or any court punished someone for murder. Cain, who slew his brother Abel, was a murderer long before there were States and courts. And he confessed, under the pressure of the witness of his conscience, *My sin is so great that I cannot find forgiveness! . . . Anyone who finds me, will kill me, the murderer* (Gen 4:13).

"Thou shalt not kill!" This commandment of God, the one Lord who has the right to decide life and death, was written into the hearts of men from the beginning, long before God gave His commandments to the children of Israel on Mount Sinai, in those brief sentences carved in stone that are written for us in holy Scripture, the commandments that we learned by heart from the Catechism as children.

"I am the Lord your God!" Thus does this unchangeable law begin. "Thou shalt not have strange gods before me!" The one, transcendent, almighty, all-knowing, eternally holy and righteous God, our Creator and our only Judge, gave us these commandments! Out of love for us He wrote them on our hearts and prescribed them for us, for they correspond to the requirements of our divinely-created nature; they are the inalienable norms of a human life and a communal life that is rational, pleasing to God, conducive to well-being, and holy.

God, our Father, desires by these commandments to gather us, His children, together, as the hen gathers her chicks beneath her wings. When we men follow these commands, these invitations, these calls of God, then we are protected, guarded, preserved from harm, saved from the threatening disaster, like the chicks beneath the wings of the hen.

"Jerusalem, Jerusalem, how often would I have gathered your children together as the hen gathers her chicks beneath her wings. But you would not!" Must that be repeated in our German Fatherland, in our Westphalian *Heimat,* in our city of Münster? How do things stand in Germany, how do things stand with us here, in regard to obedience to God's commandments?

The eighth commandment: "Thou shalt not bear false witness, thou shalt not lie!" How often is it brazenly, even publicly, broken!

The seventh commandment: "Thou shalt not take the property of another!" Whose property is now secure, after the arbitrary and ruthless appropriation of the property of our brothers and sisters who belong to Catholic religious orders? Whose property is protected, if these unjustly confiscated properties are not returned?

The sixth commandment: "Thou shalt not commit adultery!" Think of the recommendations of a liberal attitude to sexual intercourse and single motherhood contained in the famous Open Letter of Rudolf Hess—who has since disappeared—that was printed in all the newspapers.[5] What can one already see and read and experience here in Münster of shamelessness and filth! To what amount of shamelessness in dress have the young had to accustom themselves. Preparation for later adultery! For it will destroy the sense of shame, the guardian of chastity.

Now the fifth commandment, "Thou shalt not kill!" is being set aside and violated within the sight of those who are responsible for protecting the order of justice and for protecting life: for people take it upon themselves deliberately to kill innocent people, sick people granted, merely

---

[5] Hess had written a letter in December 1939 to a fictional single mother, telling her that, because there was a shortage of men on account of the war, having children outside of wedlock was a good thing. Hess had flown to Britain on May 10, 1941, without Hitler's approval, seeking on his own to negotiate a peace agreement between Germany and Britain.

because they are "unproductive," can no longer produce wealth.

How does it stand with regard to the fourth commandment, which prescribes reverence and obedience to parents and those in authority? The authority of parents has already been greatly undermined, and will be ever more damaged by all the demands being placed upon youth against the will of their parents. Does anyone think that upright reverence and wise obedience to civil authority can be upheld if one begins by violating the commandments of the highest authority, the commandments of God, indeed, if one fights against and seeks to root out belief in the one, true, transcendent God?

The observance of the first three commandments has long since been widely discontinued in public life in Germany and also in Münster. How many no longer keep Sundays and holy days holy, and ignore the service of God! How the name of God is misused, taken irreverently, and blasphemed!

And the first commandment: "Thou shalt not have strange gods before me!" In place of the one, true, eternal God, men make their own idols to please themselves, in order to worship them: nature, or the State, or the people, or the race. And how many are there whose god is, in truth, in the words of St. Paul, their belly (Phil. 3:19), their own well-being, to which they sacrifice everything, even their honor and their conscience—the pleasures of the senses, the love of money, the love of power! This enables men to go so far as to seek divine power for themselves, to make themselves lords over the life and death of their fellow men.

When Jesus came to Jerusalem and saw the city, He wept over it and said, "If only you knew, today, on this day, what would be for your peace! But now it is hidden from your eyes. See, the days will come upon you, when your enemies will smash you to the ground, you and your children, and leave not one stone upon another within you, because you did not know the time of your visitation."

With His bodily eyes Jesus saw then only the walls and towers of the city of Jerusalem, but divine omniscience saw deeper, and knew how things stood within the city and within its inhabitants: "Jerusalem, Jerusalem, how often would I have gathered your children together, as a hen gathers her chicks beneath her wings, but you willed it not!" That is that great pain that presses on the heart of Jesus, that brings forth the tears from His eyes. *I* wanted what was best for you. But *you* would not!

Jesus sees the sinfulness, the frightfulness, the criminality, the self-destructiveness, of this *not-willing*! Little man, the frail creature, pits his created will against God's will! Foolishly and criminally defies the will of God! That is why Jesus weeps over the ghastly sin and the unavoidable punishment! God is not mocked!

Christians of Münster! Did the Son of God in his omniscience that day see only Jerusalem and its people? Did He weep only over Jerusalem? Is the people of Israel the only people whom God has embraced, protected, and gathered to Himself with a father's care and a mother's love? And that *would not?* That has rejected God's truth, thrown

God's law off from itself, and thereby cast itself down to destruction? Did Jesus, the omniscient God, also see in that day our German people? Also our land of Westphalia, our Münsterland, the Lower Rhine? And did He also weep over us? Over Münster?

For a thousand years He has taught our forefathers and us with His truth, led us with His law, nourished us with His grace, gathered us together as the hen gathers her chicks beneath her wings. Did the omniscient God see then that in our time He must also pronounce this judgment on us: "You would not: behold, your house will be laid waste!"? How terrible that would be!

My Christians! I hope there is still time, but the time is urgent! Time for us to recognize, today, on this very day, that which will serve for our peace, that which alone can save us, can protect us from the punishment of divine justice. Time for us to accept without reservation and without limitation the truth revealed by God, and to bear witness to it by our lives. Time for us to make the divine commandments the guiding principles of our lives, and to do this earnestly, following the saying, death rather than sin! Time for us to call down God's pardon and mercy upon ourselves, our city, our country, our beloved German people, by prayer and sincere penance.

But whoever continues to provoke God's judgment; whoever blasphemes our faith; whoever scorns God's commandments; whoever makes common cause with those who alienate our young people from Christianity, who rob and banish our religious, who deliver innocent men and women, our brothers and sisters, to death—with all those we will avoid having any familiar relationships; we will keep ourselves and our families out of reach of their influence, so that we do not become infected by their anti-God way of thinking and acting, so that we do become sharers in their guilt and thus liable to the judgment which a just God must and will inflict on all those who, like the ungrateful city of Jerusalem, do not will what God wills.

O God, let us all today, on this very day, before it is too late, recognize what will serve for our peace! O most Sacred Heart of Jesus, moved to tears by the blindness and misdeeds of men, help us with Your grace, that we may always strive after what pleases You and renounce that which displeases You, so that we may remain in your love and find rest for our souls! Amen.

Let us pray for the poor sick, in danger of death, for our exiled religious, for all those in need, for our soldiers, for our people and fatherland and its Führer.

Pope Saint John Paul II

VICTORY SQUARE IN WARSAW, POLAND, JUNE 2, 1979

The history of each person unfolds in Jesus Christ.
In him it becomes the history of salvation.

POPE SAINT JOHN Paul II provided a wonderful example of spiritual fatherhood in his 1979 visit to Poland. There he encountered a people who had forgotten who they were, who had been robbed of their identity by the Soviets. According to biographer George Weigel, the pope said to them, in effect, *"You are not who 'they' say you are. . . . Let me remind you who you really are."* As a true father, he bestowed on them once again their identity as children of God and thus enabled the Polish people to attain the freedom proper to them.

In this, the first homily of his pilgrimage, John Paul II spoke about Christ and therefore about the truth of man. He spoke of that deeper kind of freedom. Sensing that this truth would truly set them free, the crowd interrupted the homily by chanting, "We want God!" That freedom was still some years off, but the events leading to it had been set in motion.

HOMILY OF HIS HOLINESS JOHN PAUL II

Victory Square, Warsaw, 2 June 1979

Beloved Fellow-countrymen.
Dear Brothers and Sisters.
Participants in the Eucharistic Sacrifice celebrated today in Victory Square in Warsaw.

Together with you I wish to sing a hymn of praise to Divine Providence, which enables me to be here as a pilgrim.

We know that the recently deceased Paul VI, the first pilgrim Pope after so many centuries, ardently *desired to set foot on the soil of Poland,* especially at Jasna Gora (the Bright Mountain). To the end of his life he kept this desire in his heart, and with it he went to the grave. And we feel that this desire—a desire so potent and so deeply rooted that it goes beyond the span of a pontificate—is being realized today in a way that it would have been difficult to foresee. And so we thank Divine Providence for having given Paul VI so strong a desire. We thank it for the pattern of the pilgrim Pope that he began with the Second Vatican Council. At a time when the whole *Church* has become newly aware of being the People of God, a People sharing in the mission of Christ, a *People* that goes through history with that mission, *a "pilgrim"* People, the Pope could no longer remain a "prisoner of the Vatican." He had to become again the pilgrim Peter, like the first Peter, who from Jerusalem, through Antioch, reached Rome to give witness there to Christ and seal his witness with his blood.

Today it is granted to me to fulfil this desire of the deceased Pope Paul VI in the midst of you, beloved sons and daughters of my motherland. When, after the death of Paul VI and the brief pontificate of my immediate Predecessor John Paul I, which lasted only a few weeks, I was, through the inscrutable designs of Divine Providence, called by the votes of the Cardinals from the chair of Saint Stanislaus in Krakow to that of Saint Peter in Rome, I immediately understood that *it was for me to fulfil that desire,* the desire that Paul VI had been unable to carry out at the Millennium of the Baptism of Poland.

My pilgrimage to my motherland in the year in which the Church in Poland is celebrating the ninth centenary of the death of Saint Stanislaus is surely a special sign of the pilgrimage that we Poles are making down through the history of the Church not only along the ways of our motherland but also along those of Europe and the world. Leaving myself aside at this point, I must nonetheless with all of you ask myself why, precisely in 1978, after so many centuries of a well established tradition in this field, a son of the Polish Nation, of the land of Poland, was called to the chair of Saint Peter. Christ demanded of Peter and of the other Apostles that they should be "his witnesses in Jerusalem and in all Judea and Samaria and to the end of the earth" (Acts 1:8). Have we not the right, with reference to these words of Christ, to think that *Poland has become nowadays the land of a particularly responsible witness?* The right to think that from here—from Warsaw, and also from Gniezno, from Jasna Gora, from Krakow and from the whole of this historic route that I have so often in my life traversed and that it is to proclaim Christ with singular humility but also with conviction? The right to think that one must come to this very place, to this land, on this route, to read again the witness of his Cross and his Resurrection? But if we accept all that I have dared to affirm in this moment, how many great duties and obligations arise? Are we capable of them?

Today, at the first stopping place in my papal pilgrimage in Poland, it is granted to me to celebrate the Eucharistic Sacrifice in Victory Square in Warsaw. The liturgy of the evening of Saturday the Vigil of Pentecost takes us to the *Upper Room in Jerusalem*, where the Apostles, gathered around Mary the Mother of Christ, were on the following day to receive the Holy Spirit. They were to receive the Spirit obtained for them by Christ through the Cross, in order that through the power of this Spirit they might fulfil his command: "Go therefore and make disciples of all nations, baptizing them in the name of the Father and of the Son and of the Holy Spirit, teaching them to observe all that I commanded you" (Mt 28:19–20). Before Christ the Lord left the world, he transmitted to the Apostles with these words his last recommendation, his "missionary mandate." And he added: "Lo, I am with you always, to the close of the age" (Mt 28:20).

It is good that my pilgrimage to Poland on the ninth centenary of the martyrdom of Saint Stanislaus should fall in the *Pentecost period* and on the solemnity of the *Most Holy Trinity*. Fulfilling the desire of Paul VI after his death, I am able to relive the Millennium of the Baptism on Polish soil and to inscribe this year's jubilee of Saint Stanislaus in the Millennium since the beginning of the nation and the Church. The Solemnity of Pentecost and that of the Most Holy Trinity bring us close to this beginning. In the apostles who receive the Holy Spirit on the day of Pentecost are spiritually present in a way all their successors, all the Bishops, including those whose task it has been for a thousand years to proclaim the Gospel on Polish soil. Among them was this Stanislaus of Szczepanow, who paid with his blood for his mission on the episcopal chair of Krakow nine centuries ago.

On the day of Pentecost there were gathered, in the Apostles and around them, not only the representatives of the peoples and tongues listed in the book of the Acts of the Apostles. Even then there were gathered about them the various peoples and nations that, through the light of the Gospel and the power of the Holy Spirit, were to enter the Church at different periods and centuries. The day of Pentecost is *the birthday of the faith and of the Church in our land of Poland also.* It is the proclamation of the mighty works of God in our Polish language also. It is the beginning of Christianity in the life of our nation also, in its history, its culture, its trials.

To Poland the Church brought Christ, *the key to understanding that great* and fundamental *reality that is man.* For man cannot be fully understood without Christ. Or rather, man is incapable of understanding himself fully without Christ. He cannot understand who he is, nor what his true dignity is, nor what his vocation is, nor what his final end is. He cannot understand any of this without Christ.

Therefore Christ cannot be kept out of the history of man in any part of the globe, at any longitude or latitude of geography. The exclusion of Christ from the history of man is an act against man. Without Christ it is impossible to understand the history of Poland, especially the history of the people who have passed or are passing through this land. The history of people. The history of the nation is above all the history of people. And the history of each person unfolds in Jesus Christ. In him it becomes the history of salvation.

The history of the nation deserves to be adequately appraised in the light of its contribution *to the development of man and humanity,* to intellect, heart and conscience. This is the deepest stream of culture. It is culture's firmest support, its core, its strength. It is impossible without Christ to understand and appraise the contribution of the Polish nation *to the development of man and his humanity* in the past and its contribution today also: "This old oak tree has grown in such a way and has not been knocked down by any wind since its root is Christ" (Piotr Skarga, *Kazania Sejmove* IV, Biblioteka Narodowa, I, 70, p. 92). It is necessary to follow the traces of what, or rather who, Christ was for the sons and daughters of this land down the generations. Not only for those who openly believed in him and professed him with the faith of the Church, but also for those who appeared to be at a distance, outside the Church. For those who doubted or were opposed.

It is right to understand the history of the nation through man, each human being of this nation. At the same time man cannot be understood apart from this community that is constituted by the nation. Of course it is not the only community, but it is a special community, perhaps that most intimately linked with the family, the most important for the spiritual history of man. *It is therefore impossible without Christ to understand the history of the Polish nation*— this great thousand-year-old community—that is so profoundly decisive for me and each one of us. If we reject this key to understanding our nation, we lay ourselves open to a substantial misunderstanding. We no longer understand ourselves. It is impossible without Christ to understand this nation with its past so full of splendour and also of terrible difficulties. It is impossible to understand this city, Warsaw, the capital of Poland, that undertook in 1944 an unequal battle against the aggressor, a battle in which it was abandoned by the allied powers, a battle in which it was buried under its own ruins—if it is not remembered that under those same ruins there was also the statue of Christ the

Saviour with his cross that is in front of the church at Kra-kowskie Przedmiescie. It is impossible to understand the history of Poland from Stanislaus in Skalka to Maximilian Kolbe at Oswiecim unless we apply to them that same single *fundamental criterion* that is called Jesus Christ.

The Millennium of the Baptism of Poland, of which Saint Stanislaus is the first mature fruit—the millennium of Christ in our yesterday, and today—is the chief reason for my pilgrimage, for my prayer of thanksgiving together with all of you, dear fellow-countrymen, to whom Christ does not cease to teach the great cause of man; together with you, for whom Jesus Christ does not cease to be an ever open book on man, his dignity and his rights and also a book of knowledge on the dignity and rights of the nation.

Today, here in Victory Square, in the capital of Poland, I am asking with all of you, through the great Eucharistic prayer, *that Christ will not cease to be for us an open book of life for the future,* for our Polish future.

We are before the tomb of the Unknown Soldier. In the ancient and contemporary history of Poland this tomb has a special basis, a special reason for its existence. In how many places in our native land has that soldier fallen! In how many places in Europe and the world has he cried with his death that there can be no just Europe without the independence of Poland marked on its map! On how many battlefields has that solider given witness to the rights of man, indelibly inscribed in the inviolable rights of the people, by falling for "our freedom and yours"!

"Where are their tombs, O Poland? Where are they

not! You know better than anyone—and God knows it in heaven" (A. Oppman, *Pacierz za zmarlych*).

The history of the motherland written through *the tomb of an Unknown Soldier!*

I wish to kneel before this tomb to venerate every seed that falls into the earth and dies and thus bears fruit. It may be the seed of the blood of a soldier shed on the battlefield, or the sacrifice of martyrdom in concentration camps or in prisons. It may be the seed of hard daily toil, with the sweat of one's brow, in the fields, the workshop, the mine, the foundries and the factories. It may be the seed of the love of parents who do not refuse to give life to a new human being and undertake the whole of the task of bringing him up. It may be the seed of creative work in the universities, the higher institutes, the libraries and the places where the national culture is built. It may be the seed of prayer, of service of the sick, the suffering, the abandoned—"all that of which Poland is made."

All that in the hands of the Mother of God—at the foot of the cross on Calvary and in the Upper Room of Pentecost!

All that—the history of the motherland shaped for a thousand years by the succession of the generations (among them the present generation and the coming generation) and by each son and daughter of the motherland, even if they are anonymous and unknown like the Soldier before whose tomb we are now.

All that—including the history of the peoples that have lived with us and among us, such as those who died in their hundreds of thousands within the walls of the Warsaw ghetto.

All that I embrace in thought and in my heart during this Eucharist and I include it in this unique most holy Sacrifice of Christ, on Victory Square.

And I cry—I who am a Son of the land of Poland and who am also Pope John Paul II—I cry from all the depths of this Millennium, I cry on the vigil of Pentecost:

Let your Spirit descend.
Let your Spirit descend.
and renew the face of the earth,
the face of this land.
Amen.

Blessed Jerzy Popiełuszko

MASS FOR THE HOMELAND

Our culture bears the distinctive marks of Christianity.

JOHN PAUL II's 1979 visit to Poland soon bore fruit in the birth of Solidarity a year later. One of most influential figures in that movement was the young Father Jerzy Popiełuszko. In February 1982, Father Jerzy began celebrating monthly "Masses for the Homeland" at Saint Stanislaus Kostka Church in Warsaw. Soon thousands were coming to hear his words of hope and encouragement—and thousands more listened on the radio. His sermons were not "political" in the common understanding of that word. Instead, he spoke of faith, hope, truth, and conscience. These, of course, are the most subversive things. Seeing in him and his sermons a threat, government officials assassinated Father Jerzy in 1984.

❖ ❖ ❖

HOMILY AT MASS FOR THE
HOMELAND, SEPTEMBER 25, 1983

ALTHOUGH IT IS true that Jesus Christ was sent to the whole world, to bring the Good News to all peoples and nations, it must be recognized that he also had his own country here on earth. A particular country, with its own history, religion and culture. He freely accepted some of the laws of his country, in spite of the fact that no man-made law could be binding upon God made man. By this he wanted to underline how important it is for us to realize that we all have a country of our own. All human beings are intimately connected with their respective countries, through their families and their place of birth.

Our country, our Fatherland, our own native culture, every event in its history, be it a source of joy or grief, is our common heritage. The riches of our language, our works of art and music, our religion and our customs, are all a part of it.

I invite you to ponder awhile in our meditation today upon this word "culture." I realize that it is as vast as the ocean. I shall therefore try to point out only certain aspects of it, certain problems connected with this complex word.

Our Holy Father, Pope John Paul II, said to a gathering of young people:

> Culture is a manifestation of the human spirit in men.
> It is a confirmation of their humanity. Man creates

culture and through culture forms himself. Culture is
the common good of the nation. . . .[6]

The spiritual welfare of Poland depends on our Polish culture. It speaks for us and has formed us through the long
centuries of our national existence, much more than our
material wealth or our political frontiers. Thanks to our culture, this nation of ours remained faithful to itself in spite
of losing its political independence for a very long time.
It remained spiritually independent, because our culture
ensured its survival.

From the very beginning our culture bears distinctive
marks of Christianity. Christianity has always been present in it, whether in the history of our thought, art, poetry,
music, drama or whatever. Throughout our history it has
always received inspiration from the pages of the Gospels:
Our great poet and seer, Adam Mickiewicz, wrote in *The
Books of the Polish Pilgrims*:

> The only culture truly worthy of man is Christian
> Culture: Thanks to Christianity we formed close ties
> with the culture of Western Europe and, thus armed,
> we were able to resist various attempts in our history
> to "convert" us into other brands of culture by foreign
> invaders.

---

[6] From an address made to young people in Gniezno in April 1979. As
cited in *His Sermons: 1982-1984, From the Masses for the Fatherland
at St. Stanislaus Koshtki Church, Warsaw Poland. Written and Spoken
by Father Jerzy Popieluszko*. Wydawnictwo Sióstr Loretanek, Warsaw,
Publisher. 2010, p. 115.

It was decided after the war that there would be no place in Polish national life for God or the Gospel. The young especially were to be brought up as if God did not exist. Those responsible for such measures evidently forgot that God is under no obligation to respect rules invented by men.

What is important today is to claim with great courage the rights due to us as a nation: the right to God, to love, to freedom of conscience, to our culture and to our national heritage. A nation cannot advance into the future if it cuts itself off from its past and it should be remembered that the road upon which we have walked as a nation is a Christian road. It is unwise to sever the roots of a past lasting more than a thousand years. The tree without roots will soon be toppled over; we have had some examples of that happening during the last twenty years or so. . . .

One cannot expect that a nation can abandon its past and start again from scratch. And we must not remain silent when our culture, our art and literature, is treated with contempt by those responsible for the education of our children; when Christian morality is replaced by a dubious socialist morality; when teachers in Warsaw schools openly declare to Christian parents that their children's education will be secularized.

To ban Christian truths, which for centuries have formed an intimate part of our national life, from the presence of children is to begin the destruction of their national identity. The school must teach our young people to love their country, to be proud of their national heritage. It cannot be an institution which is set up by the State for today only. The school must preserve and teach the vital link which binds our tomorrow with our yesterday. When our schools fail in this vital area of national life, the task becomes the duty and added responsibility of the Christian family.

The culture of a nation is also its morality. A Christian nation must be guided by our centuries-old and proven Christian morality. A Christian nation has no need of so-called secular morality, which, in the words of the late Cardinal Wyszyński, has no face and offers no hope. It creates a permanent threat to all the spiritual values of a nation and weakens the forces binding it together.

Our nation refused to lie down and die in spite of being torn to pieces, in spite of failing in one insurrection after another, in spite of numerous deportations to the frozen wastes of Siberia, in spite of the ruthless and relentless campaign to denationalize us and turn us into Russians. . . . How did we manage to resist the attempts of so many for so long? Because we had roots deep in our national past. Our nation could not be annihilated because it drew nourishment and found sustenance in our history and in our culture.

What kind of nourishment will be available to us in the near future if we agree to what is being "prepared' for us now? Will it be possible for us to live on the lies published, daily and weekly, by Rzeczpospolita, Trybuna

Ludu or Argumenty?[7] On the shameful way our young are deprived of their national heritage, of their glorious history? On teaching methods designed to erase certain historical events from our national consciousness? How can all that provide a solid foundation for our future? What kind of spiritual food is being prepared for us by slandering Solidarity, by false imputations and harassment of its democratically elected leaders, by banishing crucifixes from schools and workshops—a deplorable act our bishops are particularly concerned about?

All measures taken against our national culture cannot but be detrimental to our development, and this includes, in a Christian country, a style of government and administration contrary to Christian principles and which tramples upon the fundamental rights of the individual and the family.

Only a spiritually independent and truth-loving nation can survive and create cultural sustenance for future generations. It was given to us by our freedom fighters dying on the field of battle. It was to be found in the works of prophetic poets who saw into the distant future, such as Juliusz Słowacki. Living in exile, he was capable of seeing far ahead in time a free Poland—though Poland was then erased from the map of Europe—and a Polish Pope on the throne of St. Peter. Only a nation healthy in its spirit and endowed with a sensitive conscience can look to a brave and smiling tomorrow.

---

[7] Communist state media outlets of the time.

Let us therefore take care to preserve our spiritual independence; we must not be defeated by fear or external threats. We must never let poison infect the soul of our nation. Adam Mickiewicz warned us:

Siberia is nothing,
the whip is nothing,
but the Nation's spirit poisoned–
this is the pain of pains....

Pawel Włodkowic[8] said that cultural values and spiritual power are not to be secured by fire and sword, by oppression and violence, but by freedom, love and respect for the law.

You win people over with an open heart and not with a clenched fist. True knowledge, true wisdom, true culture do not tolerate chains. One cannot enslave a human mind. Hence, we view with astonishment such facts as are known to us. For example, a world-famous professor has far less influence than administrative minions. What's more, and what's worse, according to the late Cardinal Wyszyński the State employs special "inspectors" whose duty it is to see that men of knowledge and of science think "correctly"— that is, not in accordance with the truth but in accordance with the party line.

Any attempt to restrict the freedom of the human mind, which is the creator of culture, is the enemy of all culture. This was brought home to the intellectuals by the patriotic movement of Polish workers in August 1980. Suddenly

---

[8] Polish lawyer and legate to the Council of Constance, 1414–1418.

actors, journalists, writers, poets and painters understood. Their conscience woke up; the national conscience had, all along, been kept in suspended animation by the authorities. The year 1980 was a difficult one, but many positive traits of our nation were revealed: prudence, discretion, skill and an ability to work together. The social, professional, economic, cultural and political conscience came to life again. As did the conscience of our creative community. From now on they spoke with their own voice. They decided to serve the truth with all their talent and ability. To serve the truth in the country of our grandfathers. To serve our country, Poland, without any qualifying epithets.

But where a lie is officially cultivated, so to speak, there is hardly any room for the truth, which contradicts and exposes all lies for what they really are.

And so a new campaign began to take shape, stifling the truth, curbing the freedom of speech, the free and serious exchange of views that had been given full voice under the influence of this newly reborn conscience. Any attempt to invoke human rights was suddenly considered inspired by enemy action. And yet it was in 1978 that the Primate of Poland had written to the then Minister for Church Affairs, Mr. Kąkol:

> The defense of human rights cannot be considered as a political activity par excellence because surely it is the duty of the citizen. The enemies of the socialist state are to be found within the ranks of those keeping cowardly silence and not amongst those who yearn to

know the truth about Poland, the truth crippled and contaminated by official teaching....[9]

The thing about conscience is, once it awakes, it finds little difficulty in telling the wheat from the chaff. It will readily understand that big slogans and streaming banners as a kind of national panacea are empty of meaning when at the same time innocent people are being kept in prison because they have shown their concern for the common good, when new arrests are being made and people are being sacked from their jobs, when special detachments of militia are created to follow and monitor the life of the citizens.

During the recent past creative people became an example to us all, especially actors, who since the fateful events of 13 December 1981 have shown an extraordinary, in our post-war years, strength of spirit, courage and generosity.

Today our Church looks with misgivings upon new dangers threatening the progress of our national culture.

Our bishops have said many times that to achieve a real social consensus, religion and culture are indispensable. It is therefore absolutely essential to secure complete freedom for the development of religious and cultural life. A good example of this would be to allow the publication of Catholic newspapers to proceed unhampered, in accordance with

[9] Stefan Cardinal Wyszynski, *Letter to Minister Kazimierz Kakol*, June 10, 1078. See *Primate of the Milennium*, texts chosen and edited by Florian Kniotek SAC, Zenon Modzelewski SAC, Danuta Szumska. Editions du Dialogue, Paris 1982, pp.149-150. As cited in *His Sermons*, p. 120.

the needs of the faithful and to guarantee that there is a pluralism of views in all areas of the creative arts.

In February of this year the authorities expressed concern that the creative community, whose active participation in the life of the country was considered indispensable, was seething with problems. It was said that people engaged in cultural work and in the arts should have reasonable conditions of life, work and association. How unintelligible and damaging, then, in the light of this, are the decisions to ban existing associations of creative people like actors and journalists, and, lately, writers: the Writers Union . . . has been dissolved by the authorities. These decisions are not understood and are a source of grief, especially because the charters of these banned associations were originally approved by the same authorities and none of them changed anything in their statutes during the period of martial law. How are we to understand the declaration made by the Military Council for National Salvation that all associations temporarily suspended will be able to resume their activity within the bounds of their statutes?

It is also quite clear that cultural development is not advanced by the existence of all-powerful censorship which persecutes the press, especially the Catholic press (not the pseudo-Catholic papers) by cutting out words, phrases and complete articles, every true and brave utterance. It cuts and destroys what is written by an honest pen dipped in the truth. And it should be obvious that words, if they are to live, must be true. Lying words, more often than not, appear as contemptible rubbish the next day in spite of the efforts to flood the readers with papers with circulations running into millions of copies. Our Catholic papers, victimized by the brutality of censorship, will make a poor historical record. Let's face it, culture means honest dialogue and the frank exchange of views, an honest battle of words—not the habitual rantings of official polemicists, who one-sidedly cover their opponents in mud through all the mass media freely open to them.

Let us finish our reflection today with words our Holy Father used when praying to Mary, Holy Mother of God, on 31 March 1982:

> *Into your hands, O Mother of Jasna* Góra, we place the present day and the tomorrow of our national culture. Let our national life continue to grow in it and develop to the full. . . .

Joseph Cardinal Ratzinger

MASS FOR THE ELECTION OF A POPE

We must be enlivened by a holy restlessness.

THE CHURCH HAS been through it hundreds of times. She has clear rules governing it. Nevertheless, the election of a new pope is always in some sense a crisis. It is not always a dire situation, but it is necessarily a time of choosing and of change. Such was the case in 2005, after the death of John Paul II. The Church faced a far different world than she had at the last papal election, twenty-seven years before. To exercise their daunting duty, the cardinal electors needed to understand both the circumstances in the world and the Church's current situation.

As dean of the College of the Cardinals, it fell to Joseph Cardinal Ratzinger to preach at the Mass for Election of the Roman Pontiff—the Mass prior to the conclave. He read and scrutinized the signs of the times and interpreted them in the light of the Gospel (cf. GS 4), particularly the "dictatorship of relativism." He masterfully applied the truths of Scripture to that moment of responsibility facing the cardinals. In fact, he did it so well they elected him pope.

❖   ❖   ❖

MASS PRO ELIGENDO ROMANO PONTIFICE

Homily of His Eminence Card. Joseph Ratzinger
Monday 18 April 2005

A T THIS MOMENT of great responsibility, let us listen with special attention to what the Lord says to us in his own words. I would like to examine just a few passages from the three readings that concern us directly at this time.

The first one offers us a prophetic portrait of the person of the Messiah—a portrait that receives its full meaning from the moment when Jesus reads the text in the synagogue at Nazareth and says, "Today this Scripture passage is fulfilled in your hearing" (Lk 4: 21).

At the core of the prophetic text we find a word which seems contradictory, at least at first sight. The Messiah, speaking of himself, says that he was sent "to announce a year of favour from the Lord and a day of vindication by our God" (Is 61: 2). We hear with joy the news of a year of favour: divine mercy puts a limit on evil, as the Holy Father told us. Jesus Christ is divine mercy in person: encountering Christ means encountering God's mercy.

Christ's mandate has become our mandate through the priestly anointing. We are called to proclaim, not only with our words but also with our lives and with the valuable signs of the sacraments, "the year of favour from the Lord."

But what does the prophet Isaiah mean when he announces "the day of vindication by our God"? At Nazareth, Jesus omitted these words in his reading of the prophet's text; he concluded by announcing the year of favour. Might this have been the reason for the outburst of scandal after his preaching? We do not know.

In any case, the Lord offered a genuine commentary on these words by being put to death on the cross. St. Peter says: "In his own body he brought your sins to the cross" (I Pt 2:24). And St. Paul writes in his Letter to the Galatians: "Christ has delivered us from the power of the law's curse by himself becoming a curse for us, as it is written, 'Accursed is anyone who is hanged on a tree.' This happened so that through Christ Jesus the blessing bestowed on Abraham might descend on the Gentiles in Christ Jesus, thereby making it possible for us to receive the promised Spirit through faith" (Gal 3:13f.).

Christ's mercy is not a grace that comes cheap, nor does it imply the trivialization of evil. Christ carries the full weight of evil and all its destructive force in his body and in his soul. He burns and transforms evil in suffering, in the fire of his suffering love. The day of vindication and the year of favour converge in the Paschal Mystery, in the dead and

Risen Christ. This is the vengeance of God: he himself suffers for us, in the person of his Son. The more deeply stirred we are by the Lord's mercy, the greater the solidarity we feel with his suffering—and we become willing to complete in our own flesh "what is lacking in the afflictions of Christ" (Col 1:24).

Let us move on to the second reading, the letter to the Ephesians. Here we see essentially three aspects: first of all, the ministries and charisms in the Church as gifts of the Lord who rose and ascended into heaven; then, the maturing of faith and the knowledge of the Son of God as the condition and content of unity in the Body of Christ; and lastly, our common participation in the growth of the Body of Christ, that is, the transformation of the world into communion with the Lord.

Let us dwell on only two points. The first is the journey towards "the maturity of Christ", as the Italian text says, simplifying it slightly. More precisely, in accordance with the Greek text, we should speak of the "measure of the fullness of Christ" that we are called to attain if we are to be true adults in the faith. We must not remain children in faith, in the condition of minors. And what does it mean to be children in faith? St. Paul answers: it means being "tossed here and there, carried about by every wind of doctrine" (Eph 4:14). This description is very timely!

How many winds of doctrine have we known in recent decades, how many ideological currents, how many ways of thinking. The small boat of the thought of many Christians has often been tossed about by these waves—flung from one extreme to another: from Marxism to liberalism, even to libertinism; from collectivism to radical individualism; from atheism to a vague religious mysticism; from agnosticism to syncretism and so forth. Every day new sects spring up, and what St. Paul says about human deception and the trickery that strives to entice people into error (cf. Eph 4:14) comes true.

Today, having a clear faith based on the Creed of the Church is often labeled as fundamentalism. Whereas relativism, that is, letting oneself be "tossed here and there, carried about by every wind of doctrine", seems the only attitude that can cope with modern times. We are building a dictatorship of relativism that does not recognize anything as definitive and whose ultimate goal consists solely of one's own ego and desires.

We, however, have a different goal: the Son of God, the true man. He is the measure of true humanism. An "adult" faith is not a faith that follows the trends of fashion and the latest novelty; a mature adult faith is deeply rooted in friendship with Christ. It is this friendship that opens us up to all that is good and gives us a criterion by which to distinguish the true from the false, and deceit from truth.

We must develop this adult faith; we must guide the flock of Christ to this faith. And it is this faith—only faith—that creates unity and is fulfilled in love.

On this theme, St. Paul offers us as a fundamental formula for Christian existence some beautiful words, in contrast to the continual vicissitudes of those who, like children, are tossed about by the waves: make truth in love.

Truth and love coincide in Christ. To the extent that we draw close to Christ, in our own lives too, truth and love are blended. Love without truth would be blind; truth without love would be like "a clanging cymbal" (1 Cor 13:1).

Let us now look at the Gospel, from whose riches I would like to draw only two small observations. The Lord addresses these wonderful words to us: "I no longer speak of you as slaves.... Instead, I call you friends" (Jn 15:15). We so often feel, and it is true, that we are only useless servants (cf. Lk 17:10).

Yet, in spite of this, the Lord calls us friends, he makes us his friends, he gives us his friendship. The Lord gives friendship a dual definition. There are no secrets between friends: Christ tells us all that he hears from the Father; he gives us his full trust and with trust, also knowledge. He reveals his face and his heart to us. He shows us the tenderness he feels for us, his passionate love that goes even as far as the folly of the Cross. He entrusts himself to us, he gives us the power to speak in his name: "this is my body . . .", "I forgive you . . .". He entrusts his Body, the Church, to us.

To our weak minds, to our weak hands, he entrusts his truth—the mystery of God the Father, the Son and the Holy Spirit; the mystery of God who "so loved the world that he gave his only Son" (Jn 3:16). He made us his friends—and how do we respond?

The second element Jesus uses to define friendship is the communion of wills. For the Romans *"Idem velle—idem nolle"* [same desires, same dislikes] was also the definition of friendship. "You are my friends if you do what I command you" (Jn 15:14). Friendship with Christ coincides with the third request of the *Our Father:* "Thy will be done on earth as it is in heaven." At his hour in the Garden of Gethsemane, Jesus transformed our rebellious human will into a will conformed and united with the divine will. He suffered the whole drama of our autonomy—and precisely by placing our will in God's hands, he gives us true freedom: "Not as I will, but as you will" (Mt 26:39).

Our redemption is brought about in this communion of wills: being friends of Jesus, to become friends of God. The more we love Jesus, the more we know him, the more our true freedom develops and our joy in being redeemed flourishes. Thank you, Jesus, for your friendship!

The other element of the Gospel to which I wanted to refer is Jesus' teaching on bearing fruit: "It was I who chose you to go forth and bear fruit. Your fruit must endure" (Jn 15:16).

It is here that appears the dynamism of the life of a Christian, an apostle: *I chose you to go forth.* We must be enlivened by a holy restlessness: a restlessness to bring to everyone the gift of faith, of friendship with Christ. Truly, the love and friendship of God was given to us so that it might also be shared with others. We have received the faith to give it to others—we are priests in order to serve others. And we must bear fruit that will endure.

All people desire to leave a lasting mark. But what endures? Money does not. Even buildings do not, nor books. After a certain time, longer or shorter, all these things disappear. The only thing that lasts for ever is the human soul, the human person created by God for eternity.

The fruit that endures is therefore all that we have sown in human souls: love, knowledge, a gesture capable of touching hearts, words that open the soul to joy in the Lord. So let us go and pray to the Lord to help us bear fruit that endures. Only in this way will the earth be changed from a valley of tears to a garden of God.

To conclude, let us return once again to the Letter to the Ephesians. The Letter says, with words from Psalm 68, that Christ, ascending into heaven, "gave gifts to men" (Eph 4:8). The victor offers gifts. And these gifts are apostles, prophets, evangelists, pastors and teachers. Our ministry is a gift of Christ to humankind, to build up his body—the new world. We live out our ministry in this way, as a gift of Christ to humanity!

At this time, however, let us above all pray insistently to the Lord that after his great gift of Pope John Paul II, he will once again give us a Pastor according to his own heart, a Pastor who will guide us to knowledge of Christ, to his love and to true joy. Amen.